YOUR TURN *for* CARE:

Surviving the Aging and Death of the Adults Who Harmed You

Laura S. Brown, Ph.D. ABPP

ISBN: 1478274182
ISBN 13: 9781478274186

TABLE OF CONTENTS

Chapter I: Introduction: Your Turn 1

Chapter II: Culture and Caregiving 23

Chapter III: Survivors and Family Caregiving? 31

Chapter IV: Self-Care: Your New Prime Directive 57

Chapter V: The Diminished Capacity Defense:
              Holding Abusers Accountable 91

Chapter VI: Going Un-Gently: Death and Its Aftermaths 115

Epilogue: Your Turn Now 157

Resources 163

ACKNOWLEDGEMENTS

There are many people to thank for their contributions to this book. First, and always, are the people who have honored me by allowing me to be their therapist. It has been from all of you that I have learned about the importance of this topic of survivors encountering the aging and death of abusive elders. You have taught me what the challenges and dynamics are, and many of you have also showed me what has worked to help and heal you. You have inspired me with your courage, your decency, and your commitment to recovery. Some of your stories are represented in this book, although no one of you is the protagonist of any of the vignettes that follow. All of you lost time with me while I was taking off from work to write, and I thank you all for your flexibility and forbearance.

Second, my friend and colleague, Stacey Prince, Ph.D., a wonderful Seattle therapist who works with survivors of trauma, gave the first draft of this book a close reading, and shared it with several of her clients, some of whom also gave me feedback. Stacey deserves credit for having made this book more inclusive and more succinct.

Third, Naoma Chrisco, who read this book in one of its earliest drafts, and who has repeatedly asked me when I would get it published. Your faith in the value of this book encouraged me to ignore feedback from publishers that there was little to no audience for this book, and venture into the world of self-publishing.

Fourth, my many friends and colleagues in the field of trauma psychology. Your hard work, wisdom, and willingness to dive into the invisible world of survivors of childhood maltreatment, truly exemplify the value of healing the world one life at a time. You inspire me to be my best self as a clinician, and inform me about how to concretely make that happen in my work every day.

Fifth, Tracy C. Bryan, copy-editor extraordinaire, psychologist-in-the-making, and brilliant thinker and writer about the lives of trauma survivors who go on to become trauma therapists. Thanks for letting me know you in all of the many steps of your journey to become my colleague.

Sixth, the poet and songwriter Leonard Cohen, whose deep understanding of the ways in which human hearts are broken and healed has sustained me since I was fourteen, and whose music played loudly in my head as I wrote this book.

Last, and truly not least, my partner in life, Lynn Brem, who is also the web genius behind my online presence. You've quite literally built me the spaces in which I write, and have generously given up time that might have been spent in a more playful manner supporting and encouraging me to write this book.

CHAPTER I:

INTRODUCTION

This Be The Verse
They fuck you up, your mum and dad.
They may not mean to, but they do.
They fill you with the faults they had
And add some extra, just for you.
Philip Larkin, *High Windows*

At the End of the Road

Witnessing the aging of one's elders, being in relationship with or becoming a caregiver for one's aging relatives, and grieving the deaths of that generation are all topics that have grown increasingly prominent in the media in the past decade. Our mainstream culture both has widened the disconnections among and between the generations while also producing a medical technology that lets people live very sick, and very far into old age. Having an elder who lives into a challenging old age, and caring for elders who are moving through the end of life, have both become new preoccupations for many adults in their middle years. Because today's population of midlife adults is inhabited by the Baby Boom generation in all of its large numbers, the topic of relating to elders in their last years touches the lives of many people.

According to the website of the Family Caregiving Alliance, sixty-five percent of elders who have chronic health problems rely *exclusively* on their family members to meet their caregiving needs. An additional thirty percent supplement the work of paid caregivers with family members. What this means is that a huge majority—ninety-five percent–of elders are relying on their family members to provide all or some of their care, either of the direct hands-on variety, or in the roles of care coordinator, case manager, or supervisor of other caregivers. Caregiving also frequently entails involvement with end-of-life decision-making, in which the available choices have grown, leading to greater complexity for both the dying person and their caregivers. Even those midlife adults who are not dealing with caregiving are likely to have some kind of relationship to the aging process of the elders in their lives.

There are many complications inherent in these tasks of interfacing with an elder's end-of-life experiences. For those adults who are pursuing relationships with and/or becoming caregivers to elders who were reasonably loving, decent, and honorable in their relationships with you, those complications are difficult in and of themselves. Finding the time, financial resources, and energy to take on the care of an ill elder, managing the financial affairs of someone whose memory and critical thinking capacities are failing, finding the time in a busy and stress-filled life for good quality time with an elder who may live a continent away, or dealing with executing the will of an elder who has died, are all tasks that are so inherently stressful that many family members in caregiver roles find themselves experiencing bouts of depression or anxiety as well as their own chronic health problems. Family members who are not caregiving may find themselves worried that they are not doing enough, or may experience sadness or guilt for not spending as much time as they would like with an elder.

There is a group of adults whose dilemmas in dealing with the aging, illness, and death of elders are complex beyond the norm. This book is for those folks—for adults raised in families that were frightening, confusing, dangerous, sometimes criminal in their treatment of their children. The elders in these families are not the wise, sweet older persons of *Tuesdays with Morrie* or *The Delaney Sisters' First 100 Years*. They are, instead, people who, as young adults tasked with the care of children, behaved in vicious, venal, abusive, and/or neglectful ways to those children. You are those children, grown into adults confronted with cultural and social demands to relate to those elders, and sometimes to step into the caregiver role. For this group of today's adults and potential family caregivers, there was no "home sweet home" in childhood. Home was the place that you somehow survived, escaped from however you could, and feared being pulled back to. Home, and the family that lived there, was a place where you learned painful and distorted lessons that you may have spent decades unlearning.

These were lying lessons that taught you that you have no value except to please adults or reduce their tension, no right to the integrity of your body, no right to see yourself as lovable.

Adult survivors of childhood trauma and maltreatment dealing with the illness, aging, and death of elders who harmed you, emotionally and/or physically are presented with emotional tasks for which nothing else in your life has prepared you. Worse, no one else seems to have thought about how to advise you. There is a very loud silence surrounding this intersection of normative midlife dilemmas with a history of childhood maltreatment.

The very abuse and neglect and crazy-making that adult survivors encountered in childhood at the hands of their elders add to the confusion, uncertainty, and complexity that emerge as those elders approach the end of their lives. How can you choose to spend your precious time with an elder who still calls you the terrible names that she called you when you were five? How do you function as a family caregiver for an ill and aging family member who repeatedly did you harm at the most vulnerable times of your own life? How can you grieve the loss of someone whose role in your life was so damaging and dangerous?

Many adult survivors have gone to therapy, or in various other ways tried to go on with their lives so as not to be haunted or controlled by the psychological ghosts of abusive relatives past. You, the adult survivor, may have told yourself and the people around you that you're over "it" (the abuse or maltreatment), that you've forgiven or forgotten and gone on. You might be right—and you haven't encountered this set of problems before. You are probably surprised by the depth and intensity of feelings, and the swirl of confusion being evoked by the imminence of this particular life passage. Many of you didn't expect yourselves to live long enough to deal with abusive elder coming to the end of their lives. How do you respond to the societal and inner pressures to treat this white-haired frail person as if she or he had never beaten you bloody, violated you sexually, screamed invective into your ears, left you in a cold house with no food for days on end?

Because so many adult survivors whose paths have crossed mine have struggled with not knowing how to understand the resurfacing of old wounds as the people who harmed them grow old and move toward death,

I have come to realize the need for a book such as this one. This is a book about relating to elders, caregiving, and death for people whose personal childhood story was a horror movie, not a Hallmark card. There are some moderately graphic descriptions of these horror movies in this book, not because I want to shock you or retrigger your trauma. Rather, it is important to know that you are not alone, neither in your childhood experiences nor in the dilemmas with which you are now faced.

Some Notes About Terminology

I will refer to "adult survivors" or "survivors" to mean anyone who, as a child, was a target of maltreatment, abuse or neglect from elders for whatever reason. I also include in this group those persons whose experiences were more subtly abusive or neglectful; in other words, all of you whose experiences were of being raised in conditions of some degree of emotional, physical, sexual, and/or spiritual unsafety. The elders who were the sources of this pain have included parents and parent-figures, grandparents, uncles and aunts, as well as significantly older siblings or cousins. I will use the term "elders" or "elder family member" to refer generically to older relatives with whom you are relating or whose care has now become your responsibility.

These parameters of my definition make you a very heterogeneous group of people, with a range of challenges in your life. It's different to have been raised by a mentally ill or chronically depressed parent in the days before effective psychotropic medications than to be raised by a pedophilic parent who shared you with his partners in crime for sexual purposes. Both circumstances were very hard, but the child of the depressed person will likely not blame her or his parent, and may have more ambivalent feelings than does the child raised by a pedophile. Not all of the abusive or very difficult elders in the lives of adult survivors were the survivors' parents, although many of these problematic adults occupied parental or caretaking roles to the child you were. Ultimately, these distinctions aren't as important as what you share–the experience of not being adequately cared for, of being unsafe emotionally and or physically, in childhood, and now the pressure to engage with the elder's end-of-life needs and experiences.

All adult survivors do have one terrible thing in common. Intentionally or negligently, the adults who raised you broke the most basic contract that adult humans have with children—the agreement to care for, protect, and nurture you safely into adulthood, putting their own needs secondary to those of the child you were. This contract is one that is bred into the genes of the human species. It was necessary for our species' survival. Breaking the contract to care for infants and children is an enormous violation of what it fundamentally means to be human, and it is why these violations have such large effects on the children who are treated in these less-than-human ways.

I will use the term "abuse" to cover a very broad range of behaviors that violate the mind, body, safety, and/or spirit of a child. This includes sexual contact of any kind, physical violence, verbal and psychological abuse, neglect, exploitation of the child for financial or other gain, and other unspecified failures of appropriate care that occurred on a regular basis. The term "abuse" does not imply the intent of the adult doing the actions, but rather the effect of those actions on the child who is now an adult survivor. I will sometimes also use the term "maltreatment" to mean the same things as abuse. I am aware that I am making the boundaries of this definition very broad. This is intentional; it's all too easy for many adult survivors to discount their experiences because you didn't fall into someone else's more narrowly defined parameters of what constituted maltreatment of a child.

Similarly, "caregiver" or "family caregiver" will be used here to refer to a family member who has taken on some level of responsibility for the daily life and safety of an elder family member, whether that role is one of hands-on bodily care, or of case management or other more at-a-distant services to the elder family member. You need not be doing twenty-four hours hands-on or live-in care for this book to be for and about you.

I have the firm belief that readers of a book should know where the author is coming from. Each of us has our own lenses that allow us to see the world more or less clearly. I have been a clinical psychologist since the 1977, and have worked with adult survivors my entire career as a psychotherapist and as an expert witness in legal matters. Born in the last week of 1952, and raised in a middle-class Jewish family, I am a prototypical Baby

Boomer in many ways, profoundly influenced by the politics of progressive movements of my high school, college, and graduate school years.

I'm someone who thinks that childhood trauma and its effects are serious, and who knows that those effects are treatable. While I'm obviously a fan of using psychotherapy as one of the tools for healing from trauma, I don't claim to think that it's the only path toward wholeness. Because of my long work in the field of feminist practice, I also hold firmly to the belief that what harms people is disempowerment, invisibility and silencing— and thus what is healing is empowerment, visibility and voice.

Because I believe that understanding ourselves is key to personal empowerment I will be spending a fair amount of time in the chapters that follow helping you to make sense of yourself and of the enduring effects of childhood maltreatment on your functioning. Because I'm distilling a huge amount of scientific literature into shorter, more easily usable formats, I will be attaching a reading list to the end of this book if you'd like to learn more about any of the topics I cover rather than citing to readings in the text. I'll do my best to keep this list updated on-line on this book's web page.

Like any author, I have picked and chosen from what I consider to be the most helpful scientific literature to inform what I write. However, psychological science, like that in all fields, is constantly changing and growing—so please remember to use your own critical thinking and judgment to evaluate the usefulness of the suggestions I'll be making, as not all mental health professionals will agree with all of my opinions.

Above all, know that what I write here is meant to evoke, nourish, and strengthen you own inner wisdom. I'll keep asking you to identify what is the one powerful thing you can do when you're feeling stuck and confused, so that you get into the habit of self-empowerment. The reason why adult survivors struggle with relationships, caregiving and end-of-life engagements with abusive elders is that somewhere inside of themselves they can sense that these are risky situations. What follows is not meant to substitute for your wisdom. Rather, it is to help that wisdom to become loud enough that you listen to yourself, and make this a healing passage in your life. My hope is that when you're finished with this book you will feel more empowered to make this encounter with an abusive elder's aging and end-of-life experience into an opportunity for the thing we psychologists call post-traumatic growth, the transformation of pain into something healing and nourishing to the survivor.

And now some stories....

Not the Only One

Consciousness-raising is the process of seeing yourself mirrored in the life of someone else, and thus knowing yourself at long last to be no longer alone and feeling crazy. It is an important first step toward responding powerfully to the situation you're in today. It's the first part of being able to act today in manners that at the very least are healing to you. Responding powerfully does not mean what you fear it might. It's not about you taking the position of an abuser. Abusing someone is not powerful, although it may feel like that in the moment. Abuse is about control or coercion, and that's not the kind of behavior in which I would ever ask a survivor or anyone else to engage.

A powerful response is, instead, one that reflects you being centered and grounded in what you feel, know, think, and believe. A powerful response is one that unsticks you, however slightly, from the abusive dynamics in which you've been placed by one of the people who raised you. Powerful = your heightened ability to make choices that are about what is good and nurturing to you, and that do not violate your integrity and values. Power = liberating yourself from the rules that confined and paralyzed you in your relationships with the adults who harmed you as a child, giving you freedom of movement, physical, emotional, and spiritual.

The vignettes that appear here and throughout this volume to illustrate the points I'm making are based on stories I've heard in my thirty-plus years of work as a psychotherapist and consultant. They are almost always an amalgam of tales told me by two or three or more of the people whose therapy I have been honored to be a part of. I have carefully changed names, genders, and other identifying markers whenever I thought that how I described a character might remind a particular person of her or his story. Some of these stories are ones told to me by friends and colleagues who are survivors as well. If you think you recognize yourself here it is not because you have sat in my therapy office, although if you did you've contributed everything to my understanding of this topic. You recognize yourself because some of these stories are so common for adult survivors that, when specific details are stripped away, the themes resonate loudly for many of you.

Once Upon a Time

Annaliese's mother, Sylvia, had an untreated psychiatric disorder when Annaliese was a child. During many of her psychotic episodes, Sylvia would beat Annaliese and smother the child with her hands and pillows, screaming delusionally that she had to kill Annaliese before the girl could kill her. It's taken Annaliese years of therapy to recover some from these hundreds of terrifying experiences at her mother's hands, and she has had as little as possible to do with her mom, even moving across the continent to create her adult life. But this evening when she came home from work there was a call on her voicemail: "I'm the hospital social worker at University Hospital, calling about Sylvia Robinson. You are listed as her next of kin, and she's been admitted with a stroke. We'll need to discuss her long-term care needs for after we discharge her." Annaliese sinks to the floor, phone in hand, crying and panicked. Her husband holds her, but she feels inconsolable. "She's tracked me down again.

Marty's father, Steve, sexually abused him for many years. Nighttimes in Marty's childhood home were a nightmare of his father's penis being forced into his mouth and anus. Now Steve is in a dementia care facility. His mother, who he has never told about the sexual abuse, pressures him to visit his dad. Marty stays away because the one time he did go to visit, his father, disinhibited by the dementia, began to grope him, striking terror in Marty's heart. Marty feels guilty and frightened and alone, just as he did when he was a child. He starts to have nightmares again. He tells his wife, "I know he's just a sick sad old man, but the fact that he can't control himself any more scares me. I don't want to tell my mom about this now, but how do I explain that I've stopped coming to visit?"

Deb's father Owen shamed and humiliated her repeatedly in her childhood and young adult years. The verbal abuse only stopped when Deb cut off all communication with him when she was in her thirties. Now Owen is widowed, ill and aging, and her two younger sisters, who coped with their own similar experience of verbal and psychological abuse by becoming very religious, wonder why she can't just "forgive and forget" so that she can help them out with caring for him. Deb has tried to find a way to put the abuse aside and be a good family member. The one time she visited Owen she had a migraine for a week afterwards, and her partner has put her foot down about Deb visiting again. This has increased conflicts between the sisters, who were already unhappy that Deb is lesbian, and Deb's partner, who wants them to support Deb having a boundary. Deb feels caught in the middle again, wanting to please everyone and able to please no one. Her migraines are worse, and she's missing days at work because of them.

John is the caregiver for his twenty-years older half brother Alex, who is now disabled by diabetes and asthma, and needs daily care. Alex beat and bullied John repeatedly after their father died when John was two and Alex became the "man of the house." He still gets violent with John from time to time. John is afraid to fight back and defend himself because he doesn't want to be accused of elder abuse, something Alex threatened to do the one time John pushed Alex off him. John is a teacher, and he's afraid that an abuse accusation would affect his job. The two live together in a small house left to John in his father's will with the understanding that he would take Alex in when the time came. He feels trapped and anxious, and has been putting on weight because food is the only thing that stills his anxiety.

Marjorie's aging aunt Sharon had been sober for thirty years when she moved into Marjorie's home after a heart attack left her severely restricted in her abilities to do her usual activities. Now Marjorie thinks that Aunt Sharon is sneaking alcohol into the house after her trips to the senior day center. In fact, when she listens to her own inner wisdom, she knows that Sharon is drinking again. Sharon is certainly becoming meaner and harder to deal with even if it's not because she's drinking. Marjorie wonders about long-term brain damage from all the alcohol Sharon drank. She's always been Sharon's favorite niece, and they had shared being in Twelve-Step programs. The other nieces live far away, and don't understand what alcoholism is about the way that Marjorie, who's been clean and sober for fifteen years, does. Marjorie feels guilty about not trusting her aunt. Sharon was her rock in her childhood, offering her sanctuary from her verbally and physically abusive parents. Marjorie is surprised at her feelings. She had dealt with her resentments toward Sharon for having introduced her to alcohol at the ripe old age of 13 back when she was doing her own first round of Twelve-Step work, and Sharon had made a real and heart-felt amends. But lately it's feeling a lot like living with her parents again. Marge is noticing herself having fond thoughts about what just one "cold one" would do for her distress. She knows she needs to get to an AA meeting, but with what time? Sharon can't be left alone for long.

Leo's father physically, sexually, and emotionally abused him. When his father finally died just before Leo's fortieth birthday, he expected to feel relief. Instead, he found himself back in therapy feeling more tormented than in many years. "I feel guilty because I'm relieved, but then I'm not relieved. I'm furious at the old bastard for never apologizing, never acknowledging, never telling the truth. And I miss him. I loved him, which confuses the heck out of me." His friends don't understand why he can't just be happy that the man who tormented him is gone for good, and they are growing impatient with his needing to talk about his confusing feelings. The rest of his family is mad that he wants to talk about the abuse, and in fact can hardly stop talking about it. He has become estranged from his social networks just when he needs them the most.

If you've opened this book, chances are excellent that you see your own story in those of Annaliese, Marty, Deb, John, Marjorie or Leo. The tasks of midlife are frequently difficult in and of themselves. Having an elder relative living with you or relating to you frequently as you care for her or him can be a marvelous closing of the circle of care, when and if the two of you have a good relationship, or have learned how to live side-by-side as the adults you are today. Time spent with elders can be a chance to learn family heritage, to gain access to cultural experiences. How many of us are glad that we got an elder's great recipe for a special ethnic dish or their short-cut strategy for soldering circuits because we were hanging out with those elders in the last years of their lives?

For some people, however, the reversal of roles, and the reinstatement of old, problematic dynamics are stressful for all parties. Even when one is not a caregiver to an elder, there are often shifts between who is cared for and perceived as vulnerable, and who gives care, as one party in a relationship ages. This shift of the rules about who's responsible for what and who worries about whom can be disruptive emotionally and is not infrequently a source of conflict between the generations. This type of stress arising from the reversal of roles can occur when families are simply normal in their quirks. It is heightened and worsened when your elder is not just difficult, but was a source of trauma, pain, and danger when you were little. The elders who abused you when you were young often continue to have the psychological power to evoke the feelings of helplessness and fear that you experienced when you lived with them. Here's an important truth that you may not yet realize. *You have the power today to respond differently to those people and feelings.* This book aims to help you get that power.

What's Normal?

One thing that adult survivors of childhood maltreatment often have little to no information about is what constitutes normal. They think that the distress that they are feeling and the problems they are encountering in various life tasks—relationships, parenting, work—are simply what everyone else has to deal with. They think it's normal for adults to treat children like objects, and to expect children to be more mature and altruistic than adults. Many survivors do not fully grasp that these are the rules of a parallel universe in which everything that is false is true only in that other quadrant of the galaxy.

I have been struck time and again by how frequently many adult survivors who are smart, capable people tolerate conditions in their lives that non-survivors would find horrific and avoid like the plague. This seems to happen simply because the survivor has little accurate emotional information about what is reasonable to deal with. Or a survivor is doing and feeling something that is so normal as to be at the center of the bell-shaped curve- like asking someone passing by the sink to get them a glass of water, instead of getting up to get it themselves- but thinks that they are being outrageous or foolish or mean or lazy or, worst word of all, selfish. The topsy-turvy rules that run the families in which kids get abused make night into day, up into down, and children into objects rather than cherished humans.

This inability to know what constitutes normal should be no surprise either to adult survivors or those of us who work with them as therapists. The early experiences of adult survivors have been anything but normal. The families in which you were raised were full of violations of the most basic norms of relationships between adults and children. Aside from depictions of families in the media, or snatches gleaned from visits to the homes of friends, many adult survivors have had little experience and information about normal. On any week in my therapy practice I will likely hear the question, "Is this normal?" a dozen times. Each time I ask the client if s/he thinks it's okay for other people I get an answer in the affirmative. I then invite my client to conclude that yes, this is probably normal, since lots of other people are allowed to do whatever it is. I frequently run into this adult survivor's incredulous relief, and mild disbelief, that s/he may be simply human, and not a monster, for having wants, needs, and feelings, although s/he will then often also try to convince me that s/he is the exception to the rule of what humans are allowed to want, need and feel.

So let's talk about normal for a moment. One normal set of difficulties that are common for midlife adults relating to elders occurs simply because of the large number of role reversals that occur in relationships with elders. Role reversals are exactly what they sound like. Instead of parent ensuring that the child is eating correctly, the now-grown child is trying to make sure that the aging parent is eating enough. The parent now feels like the kid; the kid now feels like the parent. It's a strange situation in which to find yourself.

Caregiving aggravates this strangeness, but it's likely to be present simply due to the normal effects of aging on some people's functioning and interpersonal styles. Not all elders become more dependent over time, but the physical and cognitive realities of normal aging mean that many elders do require more support simply to live their lives, even when they are well and cognitively functional. Thus the weirdness of role reversals ensues. If your loving mother hassled you about keeping your room clean when you were fifteen, it was part of adolescence. You didn't like it, but you figured out how to live with it because, as she frequently told you then, it was her house. More importantly, she took good care of you in all of the ways a child should expect. But if she hassles you about cleanliness today when you're fifty-six and she's eighty and living in *your* house, something feels fundamentally wrong because you're an adult now, and it's your house, not hers—and the unspoken feelings of that fifteen year old ("Stop trying to control me, Mom!") may show up from what feels like nowhere to complicate life in the here-and-now.

That's a good example of what's normal—it's uncomfortable and stressful, but it's not something that threatens your sense of safety. When each visit to your beloved ninety year old second cousin is replete with his unsolicited advice about how to live your life, it's probably not as charming to your sixty year old self as it was when you were twelve and he was in his early forties and you felt cool because he hung out with you and talked to you like you were already an adult. This, too, is normal. The roles and patterns of relationships that are perfectly fine ones sometimes outlive their value, and can be irritating for a midlife adult to figure out how to handle gracefully.

When you were seventeen, it was your dad telling you that he was worried about your ability to drive safely. Today, when you find yourself agonizing over how to confront him about how dangerous his driving has become as his vision and reaction time deteriorate, you have some empathy for the position he was in fifty years ago. You wonder how the man who used to have such good judgment about driving safety now appears willing to throw caution to the wind. You try to figure out how you're going to get him to his physician and get his eyes examined so that the doctor will pull his driver's license. You don't want to take away his autonomy any more than you wanted him to take yours. Again, stressful and worrisome, since you don't want him to get into an accident and hurt himself or someone else. He's a kind and decent person who, when you did have your first fender-bender, never shamed you about it.

All of this worry and confusion, that's all normal in relationships with elders in our families. There are conflicts and differences in reasonably healthy families, and there is also love, respect, and care at the core. In normal families the midlife adults are trying to balance having time with the elder they love against trying not to swoop in and take control when they see that elder's capacities changing. They are grieving in advance the loss of someone they love as they watch various abilities leave that person over time.

Family caregiving is also normally wearing, physically demanding and emotionally draining. If you are caring for a person with dementia who becomes more confused and agitated at night, you may have had little good sleep for months or years. If you are working, raising children, and also driving an elder around to healthcare appointments or the adult day center because she or he doesn't have a driver's license anymore, there is little time for rest, exercise, a quiet evening with friends or significant other. If you are managing the financial affairs of an elder who has been conned into subscribing to sixty magazines or taking out an unnecessary high interest home equity loan it's hard to also find time to do your own taxes or pay your own bills. Watching an elder become ill and lose capacities of mind or body is saddening. When the uncle who taught you chess can no longer remember how to move the rook on the board, something important in your life is lost, drop by drop, day by day. Family caregiving, in normal circumstances, is like being a parent—a hard thing, a good thing, a loving act, a source of stress, a cause of conflict, a wellspring of inspiration. All of that is normal.

What's Not So Normal

The emotional and physical tasks inherent in relating to or becoming a family caregiver to an elder become exponentially more complex when the one you are dealing with perpetrated abuse on you during your childhood, or was problematic, neglectful, or below the standards for good behavior in other ways when you were young. That elder need not have hit you or sexually abused you to have wounded your psyche. S/he may have discounted your needs and feelings repeatedly, conveyed the message that you were only worthwhile if you made her or him look good with your school or other performance. Or s/he told you that you were worthless and a burden, and that your appearance in the world ruined her or his life somehow. S/he may have made work, addiction, or politics so much more important than you were that s/he allowed you to be emotionally swept under the rug, over and over again.

As an adult survivor relating to or caring for abusive elders, you have been in the land of not-normal since you were little. But usually you don't know that until you grow up, and sometimes not even then. Many survivors have a superficial, intellectualized comprehension of the degree to which your growing-up experiences deviated from normal, yet still rationalize and excuse the behaviors of the elders who raised you. After all when we're kids, what's usual in our families is what we think is the norm. How many people in good-enough families have gone for a sleep-over to a friend's home when they were ten and been shocked by what this other family did or did not do that violated the norms of their own homes? So the adult survivor has had little or no normal as a reference point.

Today's phase of life is no more likely to be normal for the survivor than was childhood. When the mother who hassled you about cleaning your room also beat you, when the father who set limits on your driving also was the parent who got drunk and left you waiting at daycare for hours because he forgot to pick you up, when the uncle who taught you chess also had you running drugs for him because you were too little to be sent to prison, and so little that you were terrified all the time—when life wasn't normal, then the tasks of relating to that elder at the end of her/his life become infused with all of that not-normalness, too. As a result, the usual books and websites for people encountering the challenges of relating to elders often don't help you very much because they don't take the utterly not-normal context of your relationship with those elders into account.

The not-normalness of your childhood, the exposure to abuse and neglect, has left you with scars on your psyche and with a host of challenges in how you deal with the world. Your ability to handle the stressors of an elder's end-of-life is affected, too. Some of the capacities that you've had to develop over the years to integrate and making meaning of your childhood are incredibly helpful to you in certain aspects of having relationship with this person at the last stage of her/his life, and with family caregiving. There are some things you know how to do that people from normal families will take years to get. You are often brilliant in a crisis. You can frequently find resources that no one else has even thought of. You know how to dig deep within yourself, to push past pain and fatigue. You had to know those things to survive childhood.

But you will take insufficient care of yourself today if you underestimate or ignore your vulnerabilities to being undermined in your care of yourself. These are vulnerabilities that were put in place by the very person you're contemplating taking care of now. And sometimes when you use those well-developed abilities to push past, dig deep, and go above and beyond, you are walking right into the risks of being harmed again in your relationship with the abusive elder.

So Why Haven't I Read About This Before?

Having a problematic elder, although not normal, is not an unusual situation either. Families in which children are abused, neglected, or otherwise maltreated make up a substantial minority of all families in the U.S. and have for as long as we've been keeping statistics and asking questions about abuse. We can also see that the stories of these families aren't new. Poetry, memoirs, drama and fiction are full of these narratives. Attend any play by Tennessee Williams or Eugene O'Neill, read Charles Dickens or Russell Banks or James Patterson, consult the best-selling memoirs lists at Amazon or your local bookstore, and you'll find these stories.

Oddly, this problem seems to be addressed little if at all either in the literature for family caregivers, or in the literature for trauma survivors. A friend and colleague of mine who specializes in finding every possible resource on a topic available in web and written form wrote, in response to my query, that he had found nothing on this topic in his search of the literatures for professionals and the general public. The American Psychological Association's excellent resource on family caregiving, whose link can be found in the Resources section of this book, says nothing about the topic of relating to or caring for formerly abusive elders. Doing a search on trauma and abuse related words on websites for family caregivers yielded only information about elder abuse. Just as I was finishing this manuscript one of my early readers found one chapter in one book that begins to discuss this topic. In other words, it's well-hidden and mostly avoided and ignored.

I know the adult survivor self-help literature relatively well, having had so many copies of *Drama of the Gifted Child* walk out of my office and never return that I've thought I should buy the book in bulk. I haven't read anything about the challenges of family relationships, caregiving and death in the context of a history of having had abusive elders. The presence of the adult survivor of childhood abuse in the room caring for the elder who perpetrated that abuse, and the adult survivor's presence at the memorial service for the abuser as well as the challenges for adult survivors who choose not to relate and not to attend the memorial, all appear to have been largely ignored.

That absence surprised me at first. It's not just because I'm a therapist who works with adult survivors. It's surprising because the number of adults with a history of significant childhood maltreatment is so high. The available statistics about rates of child maltreatment, which includes sexual, physical, and emotional abuse as well as neglect, tell us that the numbers of people we're talking about here are large. For the generation of Baby Boomers now moving into midlife who constitute the bulk of people filling the ranks of family caregivers, about a third of all girls and a quarter of all boys had been sexually abused before age eighteen. Almost all of that abuse occurred within families.

Physical and emotional abuse, neglect, parents with severe and persistent psychological or behavioral problems or substance abuse, and other conditions that affect an adult's ability to execute responsibility as caregivers to children, are also all more common than most people like to admit. While it's hard to get exact statistics, the large numbers of people who seek support from psychotherapists, physicians, clergy, and community support systems for dealing with the effects of less-than-stellar upbringings tells us something about the usualness of having had difficult adults as the context of childhood.

Being a survivor of a difficult or dangerous childhood isn't the norm, but it pretty clearly isn't rare, either. One third is not a small number. Childhood trauma is a psychologically, biologically, interpersonally, and existentially meaningful experience, one that leaves a mark of some kind on most of those who have survived it. Research since the nineteen-eighties has shown that maltreatment in childhood greatly increases the likelihood that a person will suffer from post-traumatic stress, anxiety, depression, dissociative disorders, chronic pain, substance abuse problems, and chronic illness in adult life. Childhood maltreatment is now known to affect the brain's structure and function, and thus the entire body and psyche, of those who are its targets. One study using the records from a large HMO in Seattle found that women with a history of childhood maltreatment used twenty-five million dollars more annually for *medical* (not mental health) care as a group than did their peers with no maltreatment histories. This is largely because of the effects that maltreatment has on neurological and endocrine systems of the body. It's also because it's often very hard for adult survivors to take good care of bodies that were treated as punching bags and receptacles when they should have received love and hugs. Many adult survivors have abused food, cigarettes, alcohol, or drugs, or have engaged in over-exercise or over-work in attempts to still their pain. All of these coping strategies have health consequences from which survivors suffer at higher rates than the general population.

In my more than thirty years of being a psychotherapist with a special focus on working with people who grew up with dangerous, problematic adults surrounding them, I encounter people every day who are struggling with the dilemmas inherent in being an adult survivor of a difficult childhood. At each life passage the history of childhood abuse has the potential to complicate and detour people. Over the last decade, as my clients and I have grown into midlife, many of them find themselves faced with having to engage more deeply than they have in years with one of the people who hurt them because that person is now aging or dying.

When I first began to sit with clients through these experiences in the mid nineteen-nineties, we found ourselves surprised by what emotional dynamics emerged for them. I am not surprised now. Each time I have encountered this situation of a client addressing having relationships, engaging in caregiving and facing end-of-life issues for an abusive elder I would look for a good self-help book to give to her or him to read. What I found was that the book did not exist. So I would pass along general principles that my other clients faced with this difficult passage had taught me. When I would talk about this topic with my colleagues I learned that they were also encountering these scenarios, and like me, were wondering where the book was that we could give to our clients to assist them.

After more than a decade of these experiences, I figured out that if I wanted this book I would probably have to write it myself. So some caveats. I'm not an expert on aging or caregiving or death and dying. This isn't a general book about those topics. Other people who know more have written excellent books about those general topics, and I will be referencing them in the Resources section of this book. I haven't done systematic research on adult survivors and their relationships to abusive elders; then again, nobody seems to have. (Perhaps one of you reading this book has a dissertation to write?) I've simply listened to hundreds of stories about this topic; the wisdom and experiences of all of those people are distilled into what I'm writing here. What I do know a lot about are the challenges present in the lives of people whose elders harmed them because I am a psychotherapist who has had the honor to work with survivors of these childhoods.

The specific focus of this book will be on the emotional tasks of adult survivors having relationships in late-life and end-of-life contexts with the elder(s) who abused them. This is, ironically, your turn to get some care; it is your turn to have your needs, feelings, and welfare taken into account in the relationship with the elder who harmed you. It's your turn because you have the power to make that so.

I won't be directly addressing issues for adult survivors who are family caregivers in their families of choice, with elders and others who have not been abusive. I also won't be intentionally speaking to the challenges of people living with abusive partners who are aging. I know that many of you are faced with the challenges of supporting partners or friends or children dealing with illness, and that there are those among you have lived through the death of one of these people. While I think that some of the dynamics I'll be addressing in this book may speak to some aspects of what you have faced as a caregiver with a person who has related to you lovingly and well, the experience of having a relationship with, being a caregiver to, and dealing with the death of the elder who abused and/or neglected you is sufficiently specific that I don't want to broaden this book's focus.

Most of the ideas in this book about the experiences of survivors or the things that help heal are not new or original to me. Many of them can be found throughout the better self-help books on the market addressed variously to caregivers and adult survivors. These stories can also be found in the memoirs written by other adult survivors, some of which I'll be including in the Resources section to add to the possibilities for consciousness-raising and feelings of solidarity.

What I'm hoping to do for you, my readers, is to pull all of this information together in a way that's specifically helpful to you in relating to abusive elders at the ends of their lives. "Relating" includes a wide range of behaviors that run from having nothing to do with the person, which is a kind of relationship, to becoming intimately involved in caring for them at end of life, and everything in between. Seeing your experiences at this time of life through the lens of trauma survivorship, and in the light of the painful experiences of your childhood, is something that I hope will make this difficult time just a little bit easier, and will empower you in your dealings with your aging abuser. If nothing else, I want this book to be part of breaking the isolation and silence that are so common in the families where abuse and neglect of children happen.

Abuse and neglect of children have come out of the darkness and silence in the past two decades. Now it's time for adult survivors' experiences relating to aging abusers, with family caregiving, and in living through the deaths of abusive elders, to also come into the light, to be seen and heard. Visibility and voice are powerful, and having them in this situation is a necessary component of coming through this part of your relationship with an abusive elder not more harmed, but more healed.

Another caveat before we go further. Please remember that none of what I'm suggesting in this book should be taken as specific advice to do or not do something in particular in your life. I don't know your individual situation, no matter how much the stories I share here may resonate with you. The survivors who have read this book in earlier drafts have found what's in here helpful, but that doesn't mean that you necessarily will. I am not the source of what is true here. One of my messages throughout this book is about the central and core importance of listening to and trusting yourself. Trust your responses to what you read here. If it's helpful, I'm glad. If it's not, then don't try to shape yourself to what I'm offering here. There will be special circumstances in some people's lives that negate the value or reduce the safety of suggestions I'll be making. Your safety and your well-being are more important than any idea that I might have about something that might be helpful.

My hope in writing this book is to empower you by reducing your sense of isolation and confusion. I'm also hoping to help you to have some concrete strategies in hand that you can deploy for yourself in this complex, painful, and potentially growth-inducing situation. I'll ask you repeatedly to consider the question, "What is the one powerful thing I can do for myself here?" To be powerful means knowing what you want, feel, think, and know. A page describing what I mean by being powerful is at the end of this book. Simply identifying one of these forms of knowing makes you more powerful than you were, moments ago, when you were confused or uncertain.

Death, The Final Frontier

This book will also address the complexities inherent in the death of an abusive elder. The deaths of our elders are existentially challenging experiences for almost everyone. They are stark reminders of our own mortality, with the time between ourselves and death seeming suddenly shortened. Many of us can, after all, remember our elders being our own age not so long ago. We look in the mirror and see our parents' faces, we hear our voices becoming more like theirs. If that source dies, then we are confronted with the reality that we, too, will die. For many people the death of an elder, no matter how expected, no matter how much of a relief from the pain of illness or dementia for the dead person, is the loss of a human constant in life and of a part of who we know ourselves to be.

Most of us will outlive the people who raised us. We expect that we will mourn these deaths, although we mostly practice denial about the reality that death will actually occur. The death of parents, grandparents, aunts and uncles, happens in most of our lives, and for many of us this part of life happens in young or middle adulthood. The grief over the loss of a loving relationship cannot be underestimated. When it *was* a loving relationship, that grief can be relatively straightforward. You miss your dad, who was your best friend and who came and remodeled the bathroom during his holiday visits, your uncle Al who took you on your first trip to the art museum, your grandma who taught you to make challah, your uncle Hung who made sure that you could speak Mandarin because he would never let you speak English with him. Your life feels emptier without them because they brought love and value to you. This is the narrative of death as we all wish it to be, even as we wish it never to happen. It is the narrative of loss and grief leavened by the gifts of those lives to our own.

The day before I sat down to write this book, one of my neighbors died at the age of eighty-seven. His death occurred in the good narrative. He was in his home of almost sixty years, in his bed, with one of his daughters at his side. Although he had been struggling with the health effects of toxics exposures in the workplace for many years, his final illness lasted just short of a week. My partner and I were members of his daughter's support team in the last week of her father's life, running errands and offering hugs. She was sad, and she was also glad to be there to care for him, easily taking up space again in her childhood home because it had always been a safe place for her.

Over my years living across the road from this man and his wife I had had the good fortune to have gotten to know this couple, the senior residents of our block. We had seen their family gather for holidays, witnessed the adult children's sadness as their mother slipped into dementia that required care away from home, and noticed their regular visits to their father to help him keep up his house and maintain his autonomy. When his daughter came out the door on Sunday afternoon to confirm that he had died she was sad and yet peaceful. She had spent that last weekend with him helping him to be comfortable, and reading his collection of books related to his service in WWII. We were all sad. His dying seemed not emotionally complicated for her and her siblings. It was very sad, and it was relatively clean.

Complicated or abusive relationships, however, generate complicated, ambivalent experiences of grief that frequently surprise not only the surviving adult family members, but also those in the adult survivor's life who simply knew of the dead person as someone who hurt the person they love. Death of an abusive family member is full of surprises, many of them bad. These deaths are full of confusion. I'll address those confusions at length later in the book. Complicated grief is the norm for adult survivors of childhood maltreatment.

Another component of comprehending the struggles and challenges for survivors relating to abusive elders has to do with aspects of identity and the cultural context. Let's talk about that in the next chapter.

CHAPTER II:

CULTURE AND CAREGIVING

The Impact of Social Realities

Being a midlife adult in the early twenty-first century occurs in a particular set of social contexts, norms and realities that affect the lives of caregivers. If, like me, you live in the U.S., your abusive elder may have better health care coverage than you do if you're under sixty-five and not living on disability. Their Medicare plan would most likely pay for the psychotherapy that they are statistically unlikely to use if they haven't already tried to heal and make amends.

Until 2014, when all U.S. citizens will begin to have health care coverage, you may be among the millions of people living in the U.S. with no insurance to assist with costs when you need professional help to deal with your own emotional turmoil. Since being an adult survivor often leads to underemployment or struggles being in the workplace, you are more likely to be one of the growing number of Americans who are uninsured until the new health care law goes into effect. This imbalance of resources, which mirrors some of the imbalances in the family where you grew up, is an important and troubling aspect of the social realities that surround you. You may need help, and it may still be harder for you to get it than it is for the elder who harmed you.

Since one of the common effects of becoming a family caregiver is reduction of work hours or temporary absence from the workplace, many family caregivers who have had good health insurance find it less available at a time when they are more likely to be needing mental health care themselves. While all of these realities about the difficulties inherent in getting access to psychological support are true for the majority of family caregivers, this problem becomes more urgent for adult survivors like you who are taking on these roles because of how this relationship affects you. Regular, sometimes intimate contact with a person who harmed you when you were

a child can cue the recurrence of post-trauma symptoms, or restart harmful coping strategies like over-use of food or substances or exercise or work
that had previously been in full remission. It's helpful not to be caught off
guard and unprepared for this eventuality—and if you already have been,
then I hope that reading this book will assist you to swim out of the muck
and feel less overwhelmed.

Financial resources available to assist in paying for care for an elder,
such as in-home visiting nurse staff or long-term care facilities have also
shrunk for many people in light of the financial meltdowns and bankrupt-
cies of companies that sold long-term care and life insurance. The assumption made by the medical system in the U.S. today, that family members
will step up and fill in the gaps in care that occur when people are dis-
charged from the hospital sicker and quicker, means that, like Annaliese,
you may run into the reality that you are the only nurse your abusive elder
family member has available. *Remember, sixty percent of elders needing care in
the U. S. are cared for **solely** by family members, and the medical system does not
know, or care to understand, that this particular elder raped or beat or degraded you
when you were a child.*

Dealing with these realities of costs and access and resources is common for all family members who relate to elders, and particularly for family caregivers. For the adult survivor caregiver, these realities complicate,
challenge, and sometimes erode hard-won healthier and self-compassionate
coping strategies for dealing with the painful legacies of childhood maltreatment. When a survivor's well-being has been in some part predicated
on maintaining a safe emotional or physical distance from the dangerous
or problematic relative, being thrust back into a closer relationship via the
role of family caregiver wipes out that strategy while providing little to no
time or emotional space in which to develop new ways of coping with these
emerging circumstances.

Some of the social and contextual realities influencing how the caregiving
experience affects you are going to be unique to your combination of circumstances, and reflect your social identities. Each of us has multiple, intersecting
aspects of identity that interact with one another, and with our life circumstances, to frame our ways of being in the world. We all have a sex, a gender,
an ethnicity, a social class, a sexual orientation, an existential or spiritual sys-

tem, we all have our own abilities and disabilities. These aspects of self mix and blend in an infinite number of ways, uniquely so in each person. Those many intersecting identities and the ways in which they create privilege or disadvantage for us across the lifespan also often have a strong effect on the kinds of personal power and resources to which an individual can have access. The privileges inherent in being a member of powerful groups in a society, or the disadvantages attendant on being in a group that has been marginalized, have regular impacts on everything a person is and does.

Having a relationship with an elder or becoming a family caregiver for that person is no exception to the reality that our context affects and sometimes constrains our options. The upper middle class adult who makes enough money to pay for good quality round the clock care for the dementing father who sexually abused her can spare herself having to change his diapers when he is incontinent. A woman with the same childhood experience who is living in the margins of the working poor may be stuck being the one asked to wash the genitals that once violated her child body. The difference in effects on the survivor caregiver that arise from inequality of societal privilege cannot be understated.

Your sex and gender, your social class, your ethnicity, your religious affiliations, your sexual orientation, whether or not your family are more recently immigrated than not, your own health and employment and marital statuses, all of these and more shape the ways in which you've responded already to the experience of childhood maltreatment, as well as to many other aspects of your life. All of these identity variables, individually and at their intersections, affect all caregivers. The fact that most family caregivers in the U.S. (as well as the bulk of paid caregivers) are women says volumes about how certain roles are assigned in the cultures we inhabit. For you, the adult survivor, these factors of your identities may be sources of strength and resilience. They may also represent precisely the vulnerable places created or worsened by your elder family member's behaviors. Your many identity markers shape the options that are both materially and emotionally available to you as an adult survivor caregiver.

"Our People Take Care of Their Elders"

Consider Consuela's experience. When her father died during her infancy, her mother emigrated to the U.S. from the Dominican Republic, and remarried within a year. Her Anglo stepfather sexually abused her. Even though Consuela told her mother of the abuse and begged her to leave him, her mother, a staunch Roman Catholic, did not believe in divorce and, more painfully, did not believe Consuela about the sexual abuse. Consuela had run away from home so many times by the time that she was twelve that her mother placed her in a home for so-called wayward girls run by an order of nuns.

To her huge surprise, the religious sisters there did believe her; her story was a common one at the Home of the Good Shepherd. They became her allies and her family of choice in her adolescence, making sure that she could stay in the institution through her adolescence and be safe from her stepfather's abuse. With their encouragement, she was able to complete high school and attend college at the local Catholic university through a special program for children who had spent time in institutions like the one that had saved her. She obtained a law degree and became a juvenile justice advocate, working with kids like the one she had been. She never married, choosing to live collectively with a group of other people who shared her strong Catholic faith and social justice commitments. She was also a longtime member of a support group for women molested as children, where she had formed many strong bonds with her sister survivors. If you had asked her a year ago, she would have told you that she had not only healed from the abuse, but had found in it the seeds of her faith, her vocation, and her positive adult relationships.

Lately, however, she has found herself in conflict with all of her support systems. Her mother and stepfather are now old and ill, and so Consuela goes to their home every Friday afternoon and spends the weekend with them, cooking, cleaning the house, helping them to bathe, and getting them to church on Sunday morning. Her stepfather grabs at her breasts and genitals, especially when Consuela is helping him with bathing. Her mother continues to turn an unseeing eye to his violations of her daughter, even when he grabs at Consuela in front of her. Consuela returns to her collective home on Sunday nights emotionally depleted, and in her support group on Tuesday evenings often has to process her strong feelings of anger and terror from the weekend before. In both places, people are frustrated with her. "Why do you subject yourself to these people?" one of the other group members demands of her. "You owe them nothing," says a house-mate, whose own job is as an eldercare specialist. "Let me set up someone to come in for them."

Consuela feels that she has no choice but to continue as her parents' caregiver. "It's a cultural thing, you know; no matter how terrible they are, we take care of our old people. What would anyone think if I let strangers take care of my mother? They'd think I was a terrible daughter. And if I told anyone else what he had done, who would it help? Not me anymore, and it would hurt my mother terribly. Her friends would all gossip, and she'd lose what little life she has left. So I pray a lot, and I'm in therapy." Consuela struggles to find a way between what feels correct culturally, what the members of her current support systems, all of whom are Euro-American, think she ought to do—and most importantly, but still last on her list of considerations, what might be right for her, and what she would want.

Culture is often a source of strength and resilience for adult survivors of childhood maltreatment. For Consuela, her religious faith and her strong identification with the welfare of the poor and oppressed have served her well, and given her a sense of meaning in life that has healed many old wounds. But sometimes the same culture or its norms can be distorted so as to trap victims into submission. Just as hard, the norms of a culture, interpreted to the survivor by the abusive elder, have been internalized as a set of inner constraints that people force on themselves. This question of whether it's culture or abuse is one that the therapist who Consuela's sees is encouraging her to think about.

Sometimes, a survivor does say no to the expectations of the culture of origin. Athos, the forty-something son of Greek immigrants, had never married and had spent most of his adulthood living with his parents. His father had brutally beaten him, and his mother, also a target of her hus-band, had emotionally abused him. Her pregnancy at age forty-two with Athos was the consequence of a marital rape, and she had taken her rage at her abuser out on her son, the safer target. In their Greek Orthodox church community Athos was often praised as a good son, held up as an example of filial devotion. Everyone knew and no one knew what happened in his home; obliquely referred to, never discussed, the abuse was an open secret.

Until the day he moved out, shocking his community and generating pressure from all sectors for him to reverse course, at which point everyone in his community knew and no one wanted to know. When he talked about it with the therapist he found at the counseling center of the community college he had begun to attend to train as a nursing assistant after he lost his warehouse job in the recession, he told the therapist, "I was sitting in the class on elder abuse and how to prevent and report it and it was like the light bulb went on over my head. Like, I could see it shining. This was my life they were talking about, except that I was a little kid. A little kid, damn it! They abused me, and they were still abusing me. I was done."

While Athos was realizing that he no longer had to take abuse from his parents, he now faced disbelief and withdrawal of support from his community. His priest called him into his study to remonstrate with Athos about his huge failure of filial piety, and his uncle stormed into his new workplace at a hospital and yanked him out into the parking lot to lecture him about how he was killing his parents. "This is almost as hard as being beaten up," he told his therapist. "But I can't go back there anymore. Now that I understand what happened to me I can't even look at them in church on Sunday. They disgust me. And he scares me. You know, he was still punching on me right up until I left? And you know I never ever hit him back?"

The social costs of refusing culturally normative roles can be high. Being a survivor can mean making extremely difficult decisions no matter what your culture, and for some of you these choices are even harder. Neither Athos nor Consuela has had the luxury of simply caring for their own welfare without worrying that such a decision would come without some kind of calumny or price, and not only from the abusive elder. They were making choices in a cultural context, and trying to be a loyal member of their community in the process. In relating to an aging perpetrator there are rarely good or clean choices. Some cultural contexts can deepen those costs by adding layers of loyalties and meaning to the survivor's choices. No culture makes it easy.

Gender and Victimization

Gender is also a large factor creating meaning for many survivors' understanding of their experiences. Boys and men are not supposed to be victims, or so go the narratives of manhood that are pervasive in most societies. They are particularly not supposed to be victims of sexual abuse. But boys, just like Athos, are victimized by adults—sexually, physically, emotionally. Boys are neglected. Boys are children, vulnerable to being harmed in precisely the ways that girls are harmed. The myths of gender can complicate both the experience of abuse and its many aftermaths for women and men alike.

Sean had been sexually abused by his stepfather from the time he was eight until he ran away and joined the Marines at age eighteen. As an adult he was the epitome of tough and macho. He was also terrified of being touched by other men. To protect himself he developed a highly aggressive personal style that was interpreted by his peers in the military as being warrior-like. The vulnerable, violated little boy lived inside of the armor of the rough, tough Marine, invisible to everyone but Sean, who almost drowned in that child's shame every waking moment. His defense against that shame was perfection, which also served him well. He thought he had built impregnable walls around his childhood victimization.

But when faced with his mother's request to take her and his stepfather into his home to assist her with his care, Sean fell apart. He told his mother that he'd have to think about it. He then started a drinking binge that ended in the emergency room of the base hospital. The ER physician told him that he needed to get help, now, because he'd walked in with a blood alcohol that might have killed another man. Sean's response; "I just gotta man up, doc. I'm being a little wimp, and I just can't stand myself."

The ER physician called in the social worker on call, who asked Sean what had been happening in his life just before the binge, and on hearing his story said, "What did he do to hurt you?" As he later told his male survivor group, "I jumped out of my chair and nearly punched his lights out," then collapsed in a corner crying. His shame at being a boy who had been raped repeatedly was so great that the social worker admitted him to an inpatient unit overnight for his own safety. That shame had made him unable to confront his mother about her silence, or his stepfather about the abuse. Sean was brave in battle, but the shame he felt for being a sexually abused boy was much larger and more powerful than his courage.

If Sean had been Shawna, this experience of repeated sexual abuse would have been terrible. All sexual abuse of children is terrible, and all of it is wrong. Sadly, it would not have violated gender norms had it happened to a girl. While many women survivors of sexual abuse experience shame, sexually abused boys appear to have additional burdens. For Sean, the harmful effects of the abuse itself were amplified by the fact that it completely violated the rules for boys and men. His ability to tell the truth to anyone about what had happened was affected not simply by the abuse itself, but by the myth that sexual abuse doesn't happen to boys.

Sean's experience in the Marines had given him many things of value—a camaraderie with other men, accomplishments, a feeling of being an honorable human being after a childhood spent feeling "like a snot-rag," as he so colorfully told his therapist. But that same source of strength and resilience had also helped to rigidify his ideologies of masculinity. His set of rules about what it meant to be a man nearly killed him when he was asked to become a family caregiver to the man who had sexually abused him, and the realities of his being a sexually abused male human child became once again inescapable.

Part of caring for yourself in the context of the aging and death of the elder who harmed you is considering the many ways in which your identities give you special strengths and resilience. You need to honor yourself, and the creative and persistent ways that you figured out how to survive and become a decent adult. It's also important to carefully analyze how those identities may have also created vulnerabilities that might turn this next part of your life into a more difficult task. Caregiving is not a one-size-fits all, any more than life is. Understanding who you are apart from being a survivor with an aging abuser will empower you to make more sense of the choices ahead of you.

CHAPTER III:

SURVIVORS AND FAMILY CAREGIVING?

Family caregiving takes a range of forms, each of which has potential pitfalls for an adult survivor. This chapter very briefly reviews some of the range of options for family caregiving through the lens of experiences of adult survivors. Because no two elders are alike in their aging experiences, the examples we'll discuss here are somewhat broad and general. What I will be taking into account, however, is that the elder who was abusive or problematic for you when you were a child was also engaging in behaviors that affected her/his health and her/his own aging processes. Healthy aging is a function of the intersection between a person's genetic makeup and their health behaviors during their lifetime, as well as the social circumstances that have conferred health benefits or created health disparities. It also has a great deal to do with access to and use of social support, and with engagement in tasks of new learning throughout the lifespan.

Elders who, as young adults, abused cigarettes, alcohol and other drugs, or food, who were compulsive in their relationships with money or sex, or who performed poorly in the workplace due to behavioral problems, all increased their risks of having a not-so-healthy old age. Declining health and/or cognitive capacities in elders, which often go hand-in-hand, increase the likelihood that family members will be asked to fill the role of caregivers. Thus factors which increase the likelihood that an adult may be abusive or neglectful also increase the likelihood of health and cognitive problems as they age.

This is not a one-to-one correlation. We all know people who ate right, exercised, never smoked, drank in moderation, took adult education classes, and developed Alzheimer's disease because they had a strong genetic predisposition to it. We also all know people who have abused their bodies as well as those of other people and are living an apparently hale and hearty old age. As the psalmist of the Bible said, "I have seen the wicked spreading like the green bay tree." The irrationality of relationships between goodness and good outcomes has been bothering humans for millennia. Nonetheless, the relationship between abuse of self, abuse of others, and faster deterioration in old age does exist.

Two Stories

Let's look at the contrasts in need for caregiving, and family capacity to give care, when earlier abusive family patterns generate later health problems for an elder. These are the stories of Alina and Rose.

Alina emigrated to the U.S. from Romania at the end of the First World War with her family. She was in her early teens. As she told her granddaughters, she was never quite sure of the year of her birth because no one kept formal records in "the old country." Once landed in the U.S. she went to work as a clerk in a grocery store. She also began to take night school classes to learn English. At the age of twenty she entered nursing school to become a registered nurse, a profession in which she worked, with breaks for the birth of her two children, until she was in her fifties. She married late for her age cohort, at twenty-six, to a man who had been her friend for many years.

Alina was always interested in health. Her children and grandchildren teased her that they knew about cutting the fat off their meat long before everyone got worried about cholesterol. She became involved in a number of different social welfare organizations, always spearheading health-related projects. She never smoked, and had talked her fiancé out of smoking as a condition of her marrying him. The family took walks together after dinner, even in the cold and dark of winter. Alina and her husband were loving parents to their two children, whose births they had carefully planned and spaced with the use of a diaphragm and condoms. Both children went to college, and their elder daughter, inspired by her mother, became a family practice physician, while the younger followed her dreams of becoming a landscape architect. Theirs was a happy family.

When Alina was widowed at the age of eighty-two, her daughters suggested that she move in with one of them. Despite her deep grief at the loss of her best friend, she refused the offer, being fiercely attached to her independence. "I might be old and sad, but I'm healthy as a horse," she asserted. "But what if you fall down, Ma, and no one's there to know about it?" her younger daughter asked. After lengthy discussions with her daughters, Alina offered to meet her daughters halfway, and moved into a high-rise community for older adults that had excellent emergency response measures in place, but which created full autonomy and ample social opportunities for those residents who wished it.

As she crossed into her nineties Alina began to have a series of health problems that undermined her ability to be autonomous. After many further discussions with the younger generations, she agreed to move into her eldest grandson's home, where he and his husband could keep a closer watch on her. She lived with them until her death at ninety-nine, frequently joining them for Sunday brunch with their circle of friends who were all impressed by how she kept current with the latest technologies.

Rose came to the U.S. around the same time, and to similar circumstances, as Alina. But there the two stories diverge. Rose had never been particularly happy in her life, and had had huge hopes and dreams that coming to America would change her life for the better. She went to work in a dry goods store, and started smoking because she wanted to be a modern woman. When nothing in her life got better, and many things became harder, she started to struggle with depression, which plagued her intermittently for the rest of her life. She quit her job and married at age eighteen to a man her brother worked with. The marriage was not a happy one, and she and her husband frequently had loud, angry fights about his drinking and her beliefs that he was being unfaithful to her. Her three children, none of them planned or particularly wished-for, were born in quick succession. After the third she had her tubes tied.

Rose's English was never very good. She relied on her children, especially her eldest, to deal with the world for her when she had to step anywhere outside of her immigrant community. She was frequently unwell and tired, and would spend many days in bed, dozing, and many nights walking the floor, insomniac. Her patience was minimal, and she would often scream at her children. On more than one occasion her rage would boil over into physical violence. The children sought refuge at school, and did well academically. This seemed only to increase Rose's rage at them, "You think you're better than me? Smarter than me? I'll show you who's smarter." Her husband, whose drinking had devolved into alcoholism, was rarely home to step between Rose and the children, although he was nice enough to them when he was around. He died young, in his forties, from a bleeding gastric ulcer related to his alcohol abuse.

Rose isolated herself at home, and food and cigarettes became her friends. Today we would say that she was treating her depression with the chemical tools available to her. As a result of these coping strategies she began to experience serious health problems by her early fifties; Type II diabetes, chronic bronchitis, and at fifty-five, a diagnosis of breast cancer for which she was treated with surgery and radiation. Rose's health continued to deteriorate, and in her early seventies she started to have TIAs (transient ischemic attacks, or small strokes) that impaired her memory and slurred her speech. She also became much more verbally abusive to everyone around her, with the effects of the TIAs undermining what little control she had had over her rage.

Her three children, all of whom had escaped home as quickly as they could find the means to do so, now found themselves in a quandary about what to do for Rose. She was ill, and clearly could not live alone. None of them had the means to hire a caregiver for their mother so that she could remain in her home. Although each one had been able to become solidly employed in adulthood, their own struggles with depression and other psychological effects of the abuse they had suffered at Rose's hands had led to each of them being under-employed and earning less than their intellectual potential might have promised. Her own funds were sparse, as she lived on a small Social Security check. The notion of putting her into a care facility felt messy and guilt-inducing, and in fact Rose had raged at her eldest son, at his last visit, that he had better not dare to stick her in a home. But the idea of moving her into one of their homes filled each of her offspring with dread. Eventually the three children found a care facility that accepted Medicaid funding, and over her protests and with much guilt on each of their parts Rose was moved in. She died of a massive stroke a year later.

Not all abusive elders will have a sicker old age. As one of my clients said about her ninety-five year old father, who had verbally and emotionally abused her for most of her childhood, "The s.o.b. is too mean to die; he's healthier than everyone else in the family, maybe because he's taking it all out on us." But if an elder's abusive behaviors toward children were accompanied by additional self-destructive activities, those failures of self-care are indeed likely to show up as more, and worse, health problems in the latter part of life. What this means is that adult survivors are probably more likely than people who grew up in good-enough families to be faced with care needs for an elder, and thus be in a position to have to decide whether, and how, to engage in family caregiving.

The Roles of the Family Caregiver: Whether, and How

Caregiving for an elder can take many forms. Each form creates certain kinds of stresses, some financial, some psychological, some moral and spiritual, and combinations of all of these. For adult survivors, the calculus of which kinds of stressors are more tolerable, and which more likely to be retraumatizing in some way that you cannot encompass well, is an extremely important component of decisions about how, or whether, to participate in family caregiving. At each moment of decision-making, a process that continues through the death of the elder and perhaps beyond, a survivor's first and most difficult job is to pay attention to her or his own feelings, needs, and well-being. Caring for *you* is paramount in this endeavor.

Because the normal relationship between adults and children was distorted in some important ways by the adults in your childhood, knowing these needs and feelings of your own may feel well-nigh impossible, and is often a source of shame, guilt, and confusion. Remember that you must be loyal to yourself as you make decisions in relationship to the elder who harmed you.

The "whether" question is the first one to which you must respond, and offers you your first chance to put yourself squarely in the picture. The first powerful thing that you can do is to ask yourself if you are willing to be a family caregiver in any way, shape, or form. Knowing what you feel and want, and operating from a position of that knowledge, empowers you at the outset in ways that will help you to help yourself at every subsequent step. You need to become willing to remain open to all answers, including the answer of "No," or even "Hell no," as one friend of mine said to me.

You must be willing to change your answer should circumstances change in ways that imperil your well-being.

Many people who had good-enough childhood experiences seem shocked by the notion that an otherwise able-bodied and capable young or midlife adult would *not* consider participating in some way in the care for an aging or ill elder. But the circumstances for the adult survivor are distinctly different from those of adults whose elders were good-enough.

Abusive adults have broken the basic human contract between them-selves and the children in their care. Adult survivors of abuse are not morally obligated to keep their half of this broken contract. The adult survivor is not the one who broke the contract. The abusive elder carries full and sole responsibility for having broken it.

This is such an important and central point, and one that is often so shocking to adult survivors when I first put it to them, that I want to expand on this so that we anticipate as many as possible of your inner critic's objections. Let's start with the basic human contract. The evolution of the human species over millions of years created human offspring who are more dependent and dependent for much longer, than the young of any other species on the planet. This lengthened period of dependency allowed our large brains to fully develop. The most recent research on brain development indicates that human brains, particularly those parts of the brain that make us most human, our orbital pre-frontal cortex, do not complete development until the middle of our twenties. As human children we *need* adults in their lives to care for us and to put our welfare first until we are able to do so themselves. Human children need our elders to feed us, keep us warm enough, educate us in the ways of relating to other humans, teach us how to protect ourselves and assess risk in physical, moral, spiritual, and interpersonal realms. This job of protecting the young of our species is one of the few things that most students of human behavior will agree on as being completely hard-wired into humans by evolutionary forces.

Abusive, neglectful, uncaring elders are thus acting against not only the children in their care. They are also violating the core tenets of human behavior and relationships. There are many reasons why adults do these things to children. *None of those reasons is **ever** the child's own acts or omissions. Never. Never.*

But, says your critic, (or your friends, or your faith, or the norms of your culture) you should rise above. You are better than this person. You can choose to sacrifice yourself…and I say, wait just a minute. You have already been sacrificed. You're already scarred emotionally and sometimes physically from having been the sacrifice to your elder's inabilities or unwillingness to fulfill the basic human contract with children. So you're used to being sacrificed, which makes the whole "rise above" story seem somewhat reasonable to you. Being a sacrifice does not make you a better person. Yes, like Conseula, who we met in the last chapter, you may have turned your painful experiences into the impetus for creating good in the world. I cannot easily count the number of my friends and colleagues who trace their calling to make justice in the world to their own childhood pain.

However, sacrificing yourself once again as the elders who harmed you get old does not make you better than those abusive elders. It simply means that you have been pulled into betraying yourself as well by the unconscious dynamics of abusive relationships. Sounds harsh? As we'll discuss later in this book, when adults betray the trust of children in their care, those children develop what psychologists call "Betrayal Blindness." Survivors become extraordinarily skillful at not knowing how people in their lives are hurting them. This is because you learned in childhood that a well-developed ability to ignore betrayal was the only way to maintain relationships. Survivors are masters at agreeing that it's okay to hurt and betray them. This isn't because survivors are masochistic. It's because many survivors have a deep-seated belief that these are the terms and conditions of relationships in life, period.

If you're going to decide to engage in the care of the elder who harmed you, it is essential that you listen to and not betray yourself. Being loyal to yourself is a component of making a powerful choice here as you approach the question of whether or not to engage with the abusive elder. The great Jewish sage Hillel, who was renowned for his compassion, famously said, "If I am not for myself, who am I for? If I am only for myself, what am I? If not now, when?" Most survivors are experts at being for others, but rank beginners at being for themselves. It is no less moral to include yourself in the equation as you are deciding whether or not to engage with the elder who harmed you. In fact, it may be more ultimately moral. When you are loyal to yourself, you may stop offering others the opportunity to engage in actions that harm you, and are thus morally harmful to them.

Thus the question of whether or not to participate in any way in the abusive elder's care is an entirely reasonable one for an adult survivor. It is not merely reasonable. It is a necessary first step of empowerment. Making and owning a decision about whether it is caring for yourself to participate in caring for this elder is a choice that turns away from the abusive dynamics in which you were compelled to do or be what the abusive elder demanded. It is an initial move toward changing the rules of the relationship to one in which there is a core assumption of fairness to the survivor.

What factors may enter into consideration for you as you weigh the pros and cons? How can you ensure that you are making a powerful choice? First and most important is the question of your own safety, physical and psychological. One of the terrible and backwards lessons learned by many adult survivors in their families of origin was that their safety and emotional well-being were at best secondary, and at worst negligible, in comparison to the needs of the abusive adult. This lesson cannot guide you today. It was a lie that you were told then, that your safety did not matter, and it's still a lie today. So you must ask yourself whether your engagement with caregiving, in any form, will be safe for you. You need to pay careful and close attention to what you feel, what you want, what you need, and what you know. Rick and Kris's stories illustrate some of the issues and choices confronting the adult survivor at this juncture. Each made powerful choices, although each came to very different decisions.

Rick had overcome a rocky adolescence and young adulthood struggling with the effects of being raised by two drug-addicted, abusive parents, and was a well-off businessman who owned a successful landscaping service. He had fended off calls for money from his father, the only surviving parent, for a number of years. But when his father landed in the hospital with liver failure, in likely need of a transplant, Rick was faced with a more serious dilemma. This was the man who had let him go hungry and sent him to school in too-small clothes so that he would have the money to spend on drugs and gambling. "Would I resent him more," Rick wondered out loud to his best friend, who had struggled out of similar circumstances, "or will I just end up feeling more guilty?" Rick was exploring a powerful question—what do *I* feel, what do *I* want?

Rick's story illustrates the reality that for some adult survivors, even the most distanced of family caregiving options, sending money, feels potentially emotionally disruptive and threatening to well-being. It also illustrates the double-bind that many adult survivors feel. To do anything or to do nothing, each has its emotional costs. Carefully weighing which costs are more tolerable and least emotionally expensive for you is an essential step toward deciding whether and how to move ahead. The powerful thing you can do at this juncture is to take the time to really know what those costs are and how they feel to you. Remember, you always have the option of not engaging. You always have the option of disengaging at some future point if you decide to engage now. Engagement now is not a prison sentence. It is a choice, open to reevaluation and change.

Post Traumatic Growth and Care for an Abusive Elder

For some adult survivors, participating in family caregiving of an abusive elder may offer an opportunity for post-traumatic growth (PTG). PTG is seen as the optimal outcome for therapy and other health processes that a trauma survivor undertakes. PTG is exemplified by the ways in which the survivor has been able to transform their suffering into meaning in their lives. Consuela, who we met in the last chapter, embodies several aspects of PTG in her choice of work and her values of altruism and social justice.

Kris is another survivor who gained PTG from her perpetrator's final illness. She had been sexually abused by her father for as long as she had memories of her life. She had struggled with drug abuse in her teens and twenties, and gotten clean and sober in a Twelve-Step program, where the spiritual principles resonated deeply with her. She had also spent many years in therapy recovering from the effects of sexual abuse, and in her late thirties had a job that she loved and was good at, a partner with whom she had a healthy relationship, and a decade of sobriety. She could sleep nights, and was no longer plagued by flashbacks of the abuse.

It was then that her father, a widower, reached out to her, the only child. He had been diagnosed with very late stage pancreatic cancer, and would not live long. Could she come "home" and take care of him? Kris called her therapist and scheduled an emergency appointment. She also called her sponsor in Twelve-Step, and took the day off work to meditate and journal, two strategies that she had found to be very helpful in her recovery and therapy.

What emerged from her intensive decision-making process was her awareness that to care for her father in his illness was a final step in her healing. "His abuse tried to deform me, to make me into someone who was fearful and restricted and unable to have choice," she told her therapist. "The reality is that he can no longer harm me, no matter what he says or does, unless I allow him to deform me again. The person I am today would say yes to this request from anyone else ill and in pain. So I choose to say yes to my father, because today I have choice." Kris took personal power in every aspect of this decision. She paid attention to what she felt, wanted, and knew, and to honoring the person she had become. She allowed herself to consider the option of saying no to her father's request, and felt that as a valid option.

Kris also determined that before she went back to her childhood home she would have a conversation with her father on the phone that made clear that she was fully cognizant of the sexual abuse (a topic she had never before discussed with him), and that she expected him, to the degree possible given his medical condition, to talk with her about what he had done, so that she could close the one open loop in her recovery process. This boundary that she set, although difficult for her to stick with, was the door through which her steps toward PTG could advance. Once again, Kris was doing a powerful thing. She was not simply agreeing to care for her father. She was making his reciprocal care for her a condition of her willingness to participate.

Kris made the call to her father from her therapist's office so that she would have support and, if needed, coaching to stay on message during the call. Her father's response, "I thought you forgot about all of that stuff," surprised her, and let her realize that she had never required her father to confront the damage he had done to her because she had never placed it clearly in front of him. When he agreed that the topic was on the table, Kris made arrangements to take leave from her job and fly to the city where he lived to care for him. She ensured, in taking leave, that she would not lose seniority or benefits. Once again, she refused to make her safety and welfare less important than her father's in any way. Caring for herself was in the forefront of her mind with each decision.

Kris set a number of on-going self-care steps into place before she left. She committed to daily phone check-ins with her sponsor, and found Twelve-Step meetings near her father's house so that she could attend those at least twice a week. She arranged Skype sessions with her therapist weekly. Her partner agreed to fly in on weekends to be with her. A friend of Kris's from Twelve-Step who was a social worker offered to assist her long-distance with finding respite care, cautioning Kris against taking on 24/7 care of her father for an indeterminate period of time.

"Taking care of my father through his dying was the most therapeutic thing I've ever done for myself," she told her therapist four months later. "I was able to be an adult on behalf of the kid I was. I didn't torment him, but I did push him hard to engage with me about what he had done, and I got to hear him apologize. It felt real, and it was something I had been yearning for without really knowing it. And I got to be me, the decent human being with values of caring for others. He had lost his power over me, completely lost it. I hadn't known how big that would be." For Kris, the decision to care very directly for her father, the man who had perpetrated sexual abuse on her, was both made possible by earlier PTG, and also led to further PTG. Being herself, a person of integrity who was acting consonant with her own values, from a position of choice, was a powerful stance for Kris to take. Small wonder it felt so therapeutic to her.

Deciding on Behalf of Your Own Welfare

In your own decision-making process about whether to be involved as a family caregiver it's incredibly important to listen to your own inner wisdom, and to make decisions that reflect the welfare of the kid you were as well as the inner and material resources available to you today. Don't expect that everyone in your life today will understand or support your decisions, no matter what options you pick. Many of Kris's friends, who knew that her father had sexually abused her, were incredulous when she told them of her decision to care for him, and unable to believe that her therapist would support her in it. Some of Rick's friends, who also knew that his father had abused and neglected him, thought he was being overly sensitive. "Come on, man, it's just money, and you should be over it already anyhow, right?"

While friends, partner, siblings, therapists, sponsor, and clergy may all be people with whom you consult while making this decision, ultimately *you* are the person whose welfare is your responsibility, and only you can know what choice is the one most likely to avoid retraumatization and/or create PTG. Only you know what empowers you, and what undermines you. As an adult you can, and must, take care of *you* and be loyal to yourself. You're in a position to be the good adult in your own life—the one not available to you as a child.

The choices that your siblings, if you have them, will make, must not dictate what your choice is. This is because in any family where abuse has occurred the effects on each of the siblings, and their ways of integrating the experience of abuse into their lives, will vary, sometimes enormously. Jamilla's sisters and brothers were all involved in the life of their mother, whose dementia had been caused by her active alcoholism. Jamilla, however, made the decision that being around her mother was too emotionally risky for her. She had just started up therapy again after her twelve-year-old daughter's puberty had evoked a new round of memories of her childhood, and she was feeling shaky. She was able to tell her siblings that she honored and appreciated their choices, and hoped that they would do the same with her choice. There were days when that agreement got fuzzy around the edges, particularly with her eldest brother, who would call her and slip guilt-inducing information into their conversations. Jamilla did the powerful thing, asking herself, "How does this feel to me? What do I want?" and was able to compassionately confront her brother about her agenda to pull her into the caregiver team.

Knowing what *you* feel, want, and know is empowering. Complying with what others want may reduce your anxiety for a while, but it will likely not empower you, and it may put you at emotional risk. Having a clear boundary with other people who have difficulties with your choice may be anxiety-provoking, and it will ultimately be both empowering, and a step away from abusive family dynamics.

Deciding to abstain from participating in some or any aspect of family caregiving for an abusive elder can be a very difficult stance to take because of the two cultural scripts that it disrupts. First is the script that says that families are places where the contract to care for children is kept. This is a sacred narrative for most cultures, and it is more often true than not. But there are families that break this contract. You know—you grew up in one of them. Almost everyone who disrupts this storyline by telling truths about abuse of children faces stigma and marginalization in some quarters, including in those broken families where denial about the ways in which children have been dealt with goes hand in hand with other abusive dynamics.

The second disrupted story line is the one saying that families should care for one another no matter what, and that honoring one's elders is best expressed by caring for them as they age or if they become ill. This last narrative is particularly strong for women of almost all cultures. It comes to life in the statistics showing that the huge majority of caregivers, both family and paid, are women. A woman who abstains from the culturally assigned role of nurturing is seen as deviant in ways that men who make similar choices are not. Whatever your sex, if you decide to not participate in family caregiving you are likely to run into questions and challenges to your choice and integrity. So it's important to remember—*you did not break the caring contract in your family. Your elder broke that contract a long time ago. Choosing to make the broken contract overt by refusing to keep your side of it only makes it clear how broken it was. You did not break it.*

Making a choice to say no to participation in any form is extremely counter-cultural. Yet it may be the best of terrible choices created for the adult survivor by the abuse perpetrated by the elder in previous years. This is an important point, so I'll say it again. *The reality of having choices that are all bad in some way was generated by the elder's behavior. It is not the adult survivor's failure to be flexible or creative or willing or forgiving that is foreclosing other choices. The abusive elder shut these doors long ago.* Kris's actions and her degree of PTG are not the norm.

Rick's ultimate decision to give no money to his father, and to allow the social safety net to be the sole source of care and resources, was an extremely difficult one. "But I'm peaceful with it," he told his friend later. "I mean, he was caught with a stash in his pillow at the nursing home and nearly got himself kicked out. More money would've just enabled him worse, and I'd be feeling ripped off and used by him again."

Rick's decision to not participate in his father's care in any way freed him to want to occasionally visit his father in the nursing home where he lived out the short remainder of his life, after he was evaluated to be a poor candidate for a donor liver. "There was this one time, a couple of weeks before he died, that I brought my guitar and we sang some old Jefferson Airplane numbers together the way we did when I was a kid. I couldn't have done that if I was pissed off all the time at him. I got this little taste of the guy he was once or twice a year when he was between highs, and that was good for both of us."

Deciding to set a clear boundary with his father around caregiving was a message from Rick to himself that he could put his needs equal to those of the man who had abused and neglected him. Only when he was equal in his own eyes could he make a genuine decision to engage in any way with the adult who had harmed him. In order to say yes to someone, you must be able to say no as well—otherwise that yes is compliance, an act in which you disappear. Rick's "no" opened up the chance for a better ending with his father.

So How Do You Know?

Most adult survivors won't immediately be certain about whether to participate in family caregiving. The next powerful step you can make at this point is taking the time to figure out what you feel, want, and know about yourself, your abusive elder and your situation in life. Some important factors to consider in the "whether" aspect of your decision-making process include:

1. Where are you in your own healing process? Will caregiving open old wounds, or confirm that they are well-healed? If you are still highly symptomatic or affected by what was done to you, will participation in caregiving worsen or alleviate symptoms? If the answer is "worsen" are you willing to take on that risk? And why would you put yourself at risk in that way? Are you about to be disloyal to yourself?

2. What are your own support resources? Having good connections with a therapist, clergyperson, Twelve-Step sponsor, support groups for adult survivors, close friends and/or current family makes a difference in your own capacities. If you are isolated and have few social supports, how might taking on this job in any way isolate you further?

3. What are your other responsibilities—to work, to children, to family of choice? Who besides you will pay a price for your decision, and is that price one that can be encompassed and recovered over time?

4. What are your financial resources? Will participating in family caregiving substantially affect your ability to care for yourself or other people now dependent on you? If you give care by giving money, can you let go of how the elder uses those funds?

5. If you are employed outside the home, to what degree will your workplace accommodate your participation in family caregiving? Aside from whatever legal protections might allow you to take time off, what is the workplace atmosphere in regard to you being away or distracted by family caregiving responsibilities? Will your advancement in that workplace be affected positively or negatively by a choice to be a caregiver? Can you take personal calls at work? Flex your time? Borrow sick leave from co-workers? Or would caregiving require you to quit your job?

6. What, if any, are specific cultural considerations affecting your decision? Have you been able to tease out what is culture and what is an abusive family of origin's interpretation of culture? What will the consequences be to you if you violate cultural norms—are those consequences tolerable? What are the gender expectations affecting your decision? What do you need to do to distinguish between those expectations and what is right for you in your life today?

It's important not to delude yourself that there's a choice here with no emotional consequences. For an adult survivor, all choices to engage in family caregiving come at some cost. The powerful choice is for you to decide which cost you can handle, not to have anyone else decide that for you.

Rick was not completely free of guilt for saying no. His decision was to choose mild guilt over resentment and the return of intrusive thoughts about his hungry, cold childhood. He was able to visit his father with mild guilt, something he would have been unable to do if he had sent money and then became filled with rage at the news of his father's continuing use of that money for drugs. He figured out that what he wanted more than anything was a chance to feel okay about how he related to his father, and his choices gave him as much outcome as possible.

Kris's post-traumatic growth came at the price of redoubling her efforts at therapy and recovery. She knew that being around her father increased her relapse risk, but had put the protections into place for herself to make the emotional challenges of being his caregiver work for her. She also knew that she could change her mind at any time. A yes said once is not irrevocable. Let's say that again. *You can change your mind and modify how you relate to the abusive elder at any moment in time. Flexibility on your own behalf is necessary.*

Consuela, who we met earlier, has not yet allowed herself to explore the option of saying no, and in fact may be avoiding looking at that choice because of the pressure she feels from her all non-Latina support network. She feels constrained by cultural norms to say yes no matter what, and she experiences internal pressure to not cave in to the messages from the dominant culture. Many adult survivors find themselves in this bind, feeling that despite the abuse, they must find a way to participate as a family caregiver. Athos, conversely, got to a "no" after years of not being able to imagine it, despite the intense pressure he received from his community to return to his old role. If these scenarios of being caught between your culture of origin and dominant culture describe your realities, there are some additional questions you might ask yourself. These include:

1. Do you feel equally bound by all other norms of your culture? If not, why are you picking and choosing a norm that might be harmful to your well-being?

2. Even if you do feel duty-bound to be a family caregiver in some way, are there aspects of this job to which you can say no? For example, could you hire another person to do a part or all of certain tasks that would be most psychologically harmful to you? Examine carefully your belief that you must simply do everything asked of you all the time.

3. Would you expect a person beloved to you, also a member of your culture, to do what you are doing? If not, why are you expecting this from yourself?

Saying no to having a relationship with an abusive elder or becoming a family caregiver for that person is a reasonable option for an adult survivor. For some of you, saying no will be a "not-this-thing," as in, "I can do this thing, and I will not do this other thing." *In order to say yes in any way, you must be able to know that you have the choice to say no. A yes freely given is a powerful choice. A yes given without a no is a disempowering stance that activates dynamics of abuse.* You need to include the option of saying no from the very beginning of your decision-making process, even if you think it unlikely that this will be your ultimate choice. Saying no also needs to remain available to you at each step of the way. You can change your mind and say no even after you've said yes.

If Yes, Then How?

So you've taken the time to explore the question of whether to be a family caregiver, and have decided that you will participate in some way. Now the question for you is, how will you do this? Again, empowerment of yourself is core and central to what you're doing. *How* you participate must live up to the standard of being for yourself every bit as much as *whether* you participate. Some of your answers to this question of "how" will reflect what the actual needs and resources of the elder may be. Important factors to consider include answers to the following:

1. Is s/he physically ill and in need of personal care? Is this an acute need (for example, due to a recent medical procedure or injury likely to resolve soon), or a chronic and on-going need (due to a persistent health condition that will not resolve and may worsen and perhaps lead to death)?

2. Is s/he basically well, but frail, and in need of assistance with activities of daily living, such as eating, bathing, and/or toileting?

3. Is the elder experiencing memory problems that are likely to be, or have been diagnosed as, a form of dementia? If so, are there also behavioral changes that are occurring in addition to the problems of cognitive functioning, and what are those behavioral changes?

4. Where does this elder live? Is s/he isolated in a rural area? Or does s/he live in a well-resourced location? Are there care facilities available that are appropriate to the elder's specific needs, including cultural needs, and that are financially accessible? Is there adequate home care service available if the elder wants to, and can, stay in her/his own home, and can the elder afford this care?

5. Does the elder need financial assistance from family members, and if so, is this a one-time request, or a continuing commitment?

6. Does the elder have access to reliable transportation, or is this something with which s/he requires assistance?

7. Does the elder have particular cultural, linguistic, or religious needs that must be met as part of care? If this elder is a native speaker of a language other than English, has s/he retained her/his ability to speak and understand English, or have some dementing processes interfered with that ability?

8. Is this elder someone who holds strong biases against people from specific ethnicities, cultures, sexual orientations, or religions that might be obstacles to employment of some paid caregivers? Are these biases against the elder's own group, or against others?

All of these questions need to be asked and answers clarified to the extent possible as you explore how you will participate as a family caregiver. This is because the answers to these questions must then be integrated into your considerations of your own capacities and resources.

Kris, for instance, was well along in her own healing process and had support, both emotional and financial, as well as a job that walked its talk about how people used family leave. She knew that the care she was giving was intensive but limited, as her father's life expectancy was short. She knew that she could call upon respite care as needed, as her father lived in a metropolitan area with a number of home-care agencies.

Some people may find it helpful to visualize this decision-making process as a kind of table where you can see your answers to the questions above laid out clearly. A blank copy of this table is at the end of this book for you to copy or print out and use.

Kris's table for decision-making looked like this:

Question	Answer	Consequences for me participating	Consequences for me not participating	Next Steps
Where am I in the healing process?	Well along in recovery – abuse no longer affects daily life	Possible increased symptoms	Feeling as if he still controls me	Consider participating in direct care
What are my support resources	Therapist, 12-Step, partner, friends	They will be supportive	They will be supportive	Consider participating in direct care
What are my other responsibilities?	Partner, work, self	Partner not happy, but supportive. Work can tolerate absence and will hold my job.	None that I can see right now	Consider participating in direct care

What are my financial resources?	Good job, some savings, paid leave available and FMLA after that if needed	1/3 loss of income as leave is only 2/3	None	Consider participating in direct care. I do not want to deplete my savings, so indirect care is not as good an option for me
What are workplace considerations?	Job has flexibility and can tolerate my absence	No negative consequences foreseeable, although could affect future advancement in long term	None I can foresee right now	Consider participating in direct care.
What are gender and cultural considerations	Family is Anglo. I'm an only child. I'm not gender-conforming, but there may be some subtle pressures I'm not aware of	I'll feel in tune with my own values. Might get positive feedback from others in community for my actions	I'll feel out of tune with my own values. Might get positive feedback from others in my community for my choice	Yes, I will participate-now I need to decide how. Probably direct care
What are my father's care needs?	Terminally ill but cognitively intact; needs intensive care for a limited time. He's a native English speaker, and very unapologetically racist; I don't want to subject any people of color to having to deal with him	He will get to die at home, and I will be able to try to get some closure with him about his abuse of me, if I do direct care	He will likely die in a care facility if I do indirect care (supplement his financial resources with my own). I would be able to spend time with him, could likely get closure about his abuse.	Stronger consideration for participating in direct care. I will need to find respite care while taking the welfare of caregivers into account (explain to agency about his being very racist)

What are other considerations for me?	I need to be sure I get the support I need to do this, and have that support willing to tell me if I need to pull out. I need to remember to be on the side of the abused kid I was	I'm going to go there and take care of him. I think I'll like myself better and feel more healed. I'm willing to accept some PTSD symptoms in exchange for PTG	I'm glad I knew I had the choice to not go or not send him money. Ultimately he could have done this without me. He broke his contract with me to protect me from harm by sexually abusing me.	Those last three months of his life allowed me to finally have a father. He apologized, and I think he meant it. He was a very disturbed man. Now more than ever I know I was not to blame for what he did.

Kris's chart hints at some of the choices available to an adult survivor who has decided to participate in some way in family caregiving of the abusive elder. Some of the roles available to a family caregiver are relatively indirect or involve little personal contact with the elder while others are more hands-on. These include:

1. Financial support. One way to participate in family caregiving is through supplementing the elder's financial resources so that paid care is more available. When you have the financial resources available and has assessed that more personal contact with the elder will disrupt your psychological or physical safety, financial support is a form of family caregiving that may feel possible for you if your resources allow.

2. Finding and engaging paid caregivers. You may become involved in locating agencies for in-home care, or a care facility that is appropriate to your elder's needs and within their means. You may be involved in interviewing potential paid caregivers, hiring and firing them as needed, or in visiting and assessing care facilities. This is a little more hands-on, and involves some contact with the elder. It may also involve you in the dynamics of the relationships between

the elder and paid caregivers. This reduces your contact with your elder, but does not distance you from the interpersonal realities of who that person is.

3. Case management. Many elders are dealing with a confusing array of medical and rehabilitative services, and/or are feeling overwhelmed by financial dealings. If you are skillful at finding resources, coordinating other people's activities, making phone calls to agencies, and reading through bank statements or insurance forms, you may be able to offer this kind of more at-a-distance care to an abusive elder. This still gets you involved in the elder's life and decisions, so you will need to be prepared for dealing with that person's attitudes and behaviors. You will likely need to have some legal authority from that elder to do this kind of work, such as releases of information allowing you to speak with health-care providers and health insurance companies, or limited powers of attorney to allow you access to bank and other financial records. You should strongly consider consulting with an attorney who is knowledgeable about elder law issues to ensure that you have the authority to help out with these tasks and to create protections from false accusations of abuse or fraud brought against you later by the elder or other family members, should old conflictual dynamics emerge in your family.

4. You may become involved directly in the care of the elder in her or his own home. Such care might be intermittent; for instance, you might visit several times weekly to keep a watch on whether the elder seems to be safe and well, or to cook and freeze meals. You might do short-term nursing care, assisting with changing dressings after a surgery, transfers in and out of bed, toileting or bathing, with or without the assistance of paid caregivers or other family members. You might visit daily to ensure that the elder is taking medication. All of these forms of family caregiving are quite intimate, as they involve close contact and interaction with the elder.

5. You may move the elder into your own home to provide a variety of types of direct care. This is the most intimate and, for the caregiver, intrusive form of family caregiving. It puts you and the abusive elder in the same household again. This choice requires you to consider all of the ways that you will protect yourself and your boundaries while sharing living space with the person who harmed you.

More detailed information about these and other aspects of being a family caregiver can be found in the Resources section.

Notice that these types of family caregiving become progressively more intimate and intrusive into your life, and your emotional and physical space. Committing to any one of these does not mean that you are locked into it, though. One day at a time is a good strategy for thinking about your involvement in the care of the abusive elder, because both your capacities to participate, and that person's capacities to function, will change, sometimes rapidly. Resist being convinced that you will harm the elder by not holding constant in your choices, something you may hear from the elder, other family members, and sometimes from well-meaning elder care professionals who lack understanding of the situation of the adult survivor. The most powerful thing you can do on any given day is to assess what you think, feel, and know, and to pay attention to your inner wisdom. *You have a primary responsibility to your own safety and well-being. Remember, you are not the one who broke the contract in your family about who cares for whom. The contract is broken. You are creating a new agreement, one in which your well-being is always in the picture.*

You may correctly assess on day one that you are able to move the mother who verbally abused you into your home to recover from her bout with pneumonia, and that you can be an ally and advocate for yourself in this situation. When her stay lengthens, her recovery falters, and her behavior worsens and verbal abuse starts to leak out of her, you may decide on day twenty-one that you need to move to a different option and have her live elsewhere. That's a powerful choice for you, and one that honors the reality that this is a person who hurt you, and could hurt you again.

If, on day one, what you can do is send money so that the older brother who sexually abused you can stay in his own home despite his dementia, you can also change your mind about that on day two hundred and eleven when your own financial circumstances change. You do not owe it to him to never change your mind about what you will do for him. In fact, you owe him nothing at all. You have choices in this relationship, not debts. You do owe it to yourself to care for yourself emotionally, physically, spiritually. *You were not the one who broke the contract that someone older looks out for the welfare of someone younger. The contract was already broken by the elder. You are in a new contract now, a contract not to betray yourself and not to make relationships contingent on your inability to acknowledge betrayal by others.*

One of the common crazy rules in families where abuse happens is that adults' commitments mean nothing, but promises made by the children are permanent and binding. Children are expected to live up to their agreements to keep quiet about the abuse, while adults are never expected to hold to their promise that they won't harm you again. Children are expected to forgive the adults for breaking important promises. Children get severely punished and not forgiven when they can't keep their own word. This kind of total reversal of normal left you feeling trapped then and stuck now. "You promised me that when you grew up you'd take care of me," wails the father who beat you up. Well, you did say that. You were seven, and you were trying to make him feel better and loved so that he wouldn't hurt you anymore. You aren't bound to that promise. You can change your mind.

"Doesn't this make me like my abuser?" some of you are wondering right about now? "S/he kept making and breaking promises to me. This sounds like I'm no better." No, not true, and here's why. Adults caring for children do not have the right to change their minds about keeping the contract to care for kids. This is a species-survival rule. We must take care of children, must protect and nurture them. The Biblical story of the woman who told King Solomon to give her child away to the other woman claiming it, rather than have it cut in half, is only one example of just how long our species has been noticing and valuing that imperative to protect children. The abusive elder in your life broke the most sacred contract that adult humans have with children, usually repeatedly. Yes, that same Bible says to honor your parents. It does not, though, tell you how to do that. Allowing an abusive elder to continue to harm you is not the equivalent of honoring that person.

Choosing to care for our elders can be an honorable thing to do when it truly is a choice. But coercing yourself into saying "Yes" when every fiber of you wants to say "No" sounds like what? Right, like a violation. Saying yes at some point to relating to the elder or to participating in family caregiving should not foreclose your options. It is not breaking a promise to reevaluate the goodness of fit between your current choices and your emerging needs and feelings. Remaining open to the possibility of changing your mind is exercising your right to care for yourself, reflecting your commitment to your own welfare, your own mental and physical safety. Make clear early on, to yourself, the elder, and those around both of you, that your agreements are subject to change.

Having relationships with abusive elders, including being a family caregiver when you're an adult survivor of childhood maltreatment, is doable. The next few chapters contain some ideas about how to make this decision work for you. Your goal is to create opportunities for healing and empowerment through this difficult passage. Caring for yourself, and understanding your inner barriers to doing self-care so that you can overcome those barriers, will assist you in achieving that goal.

CHAPTER IV:

SELF-CARE: YOUR NEW PRIME DIRECTIVE

I am a fan of the various *Star Trek* series. The original began to air when I was in junior high school. The crew of the Starship Enterprise was tasked with exploring the vastness of space. They were guided by a Prime Directive, a rule that was to always be obeyed in their interactions with newly encountered cultures, and which forbade the crew of the Enterprise from purposeful efforts to improve or change in any way the natural course of any society that they encountered in their travels, even if that change was well-intentioned and kept completely secret. The existence of this invariant rule was the fodder for many episodes in which Captain Kirk (and Captains Picard, Sisko and Janeway after him) had to figure out how to deal with a life-threatening situation while still obeying this rule.

Many adult survivors had families with crazy prime directives, invariant and unbreakable rules that usually went something like this: "The welfare of adults in this family is more important than the welfare of children. Children exist to meet the emotional, financial, and/or sexual needs of adults. Whatever makes the adult happy is good. Whatever distracts from the welfare of the adults is bad. Even when a child is doing its best to meet the needs of adults, that child may still be labeled bad. Children should have no wants or needs that adults cannot easily meet without exerting themselves. Children should shut up and go away. Children should be grateful for existing and demonstrate that gratitude in concrete ways. It is acceptable to hurt or neglect children, who probably deserved it anyways. Adults who harm or neglect children are not responsible for their actions—the kid made them do it." Some families' prime directive might include clauses about all of these rules being divine will, or how "our culture" does things. Most of these families also had another important rule: "Tell no one what happens here."

These abusive prime directives represent the polar opposite of how children ought to be treated by the adults raising them. *They are wrong, and they are lies.* As discussed earlier in this book, human beings are a species whose young need the care of the elders for a far longer time span than any other species on this planet. The real prime directive is "Take care of the kids!" To stack the deck in favor of children getting basic biological and psychosocial needs met, evolution has created babies and children, as well as the young of many other species, with facial features that older humans are hard-wired to find adorable—big eyes, little chubby cheeks. We are also hard-wired to respond quickly and immediately to the sound of an infant in distress, something we have apparently taught to our canine companions as well over the millennia, so as to alleviate that distress.

As one psychologist wrote nearly half a century ago, "Under ordinary circumstances, in any human group consisting of an infant, the attention directed toward the child is considerable....there is almost no effort we will not expend, no device we will not employ, to change a crying baby into a smiling one." Humans generally want children to be safe and well and happy. Abusive elders will tell you that this was their goal for you, but your life bears witness to the fact that they were unable to fulfill that goal, and had wrong-headed and distorted ideas about what it meant. You were not safe, well, or happy. You were often terrified, in danger, confused, hurting, lonely. Those feelings have frequently persisted into your adulthood and had harmful effects on your life.

Normal child-raising is all about protecting children, teaching them that they are safe and loved, and demonstrating to them that the regulation of emotions and impulses is an important component of living well in our highly social species. We teach children to use their words instead of their fists or teeth, to acknowledge other people and interact with them effectively (that is, "play nicely with the other kids"), to keep their bodies and physical spaces clean, so that they can live well and peacefully among other human beings. All species socialize their young; I watched my first bull terrier give direction to her puppies as she taught them to be good members of the dog/human collective of which she was already a part. All species, when the parent is well and not stressed, emphasize care for their young. This is what constitutes normal, whether you're a human, a bonobo, our nearest primate relative, or a bull terrier. Psychologists call this being "good-enough" as a caregiver, since no caregiver is perfect.

The crazy-making reversals of some or all of the norms of good-enough child-raising that are inherent in the prime directives of abusive families frequently leave adult survivors with confusion about how to relate to themselves, and what to expect from others. As an adult survivor, you have learned self-hatred. You have learned to put yourself at the end of your list of priorities, if you are on the list at all. You have learned deep shame about your wants, needs, and feelings. You will believe that the price of connection to another person is the loss of self or safety or integrity or all of those things. As an adult survivor you have been betrayed by some of the adults who were responsible to you. Those betrayals have had terrible costs for many adult survivors.

One of the most challenging things an adult survivor can do, and one of the most powerful by far, is to take loving and compassionate care of yourself. This is true whether or not you ever have to function as a caregiver to the elder who harmed you or allowed you to come to harm. It is especially and crucially true when you become a caregiver for the person who harmed you. Because so many of these elders have accused the children they harmed of being selfish, many adult survivors spend far too much time worrying about the propriety of self-caring activities that many other people take for granted.

Because you're trying to prove you're not selfish, selflessness and self-denial are norms for many adult survivors. This may account for the painful reality that so many adult survivors are also exploited in adult life by partners or so-called friends, or by employers who intentionally or accidentally take advantage of a survivor's desire to prove wrong the accusations of selfishness spat at you so many times in your childhood. If your culture or your gender norms place a premium on being selfless and giving, then you're even more likely to give of yourself, sometimes to the point of giving yourself entirely away.

Being a caregiver for an aging elder looks like an exercise in selflessness, no matter how wonderfully that elder cared for you when you were young. There's a good reason why the rates of depression, anxiety, and illness are so high for all family caregivers. It's because they have been thrust into a situation where the expectations for self-sacrifice are powerful, even though they are unreasonable. If you're able to care for yourself under usual circumstances you'll at least know that you have the right to want respite. If you know that wanting time off isn't selfish or the ultimate proof that you really are a bad person, but simply normally human, you'll be able to hire the respite worker and take the weekend off, or decide that you really need to hire a professional care manager for your elder. But for adult survivors, the crazy, abusive prime directives that put you at the bottom of the heap often get in your way of self-care.

What follows is a discussion of how to take care of yourself, and how to develop a new, non-abusive prime directive for your dealings with other human beings. While I'm framing this in the context of becoming a family caregiver for an abusive elder, these matters are truly at the heart of recovery for all adult survivors. They will become tools and strategies that you can use to help yourself for the rest of your life in all situations. Rather than give you an exhaustive list of things to do, I'm going to discuss some general principles of self-care, and then talk about how they apply to the challenges of caregiving with your abusive elder. All of these principles are aimed at the goal of your empowerment, so that you can be an effective advocate for yourself, your safety, and your emotional well-being.

Compassion for Self

Many adult survivors are deeply compassionate human beings when it comes to other living creatures. You have empathy for the suffering of others that derives from knowing only too well what pain feels like. You have a desire to make the world a better place for those who suffer because you know what it means to live in a world where there's not enough love, care, or safety to go around. The ranks of social justice activists, health care workers, teachers, law enforcement officers, and other helping professions are full of adult survivors of childhood maltreatment, many of who have intentionally or unconsciously chosen work that helps them to redeem the suffering of their own childhood. More than a few of you reading this now are also such individuals. In the face of every invitation from your childhood to be otherwise, you are a compassionate, decent person.

Compassion for self is another matter entirely. You probably don't think that you deserve it. Jon broke his arm when he fell down the icy steps of his home. Even though he had excellent health insurance and plenty of sick time, he wrapped his painful forearm in an Ace bandage and went into work, telling himself that he was over-reacting to the pain and being a wimp. Only after a co-worker noticed both his wincing face and the odd angle and color of his arm, and insisted on driving him to his doctor's office, did he get care.

Surprised to learn that he had indeed broken his arm, Jon spent the entire time at the doctor's office apologizing for being a bother and a burden and "making too big a deal out of it." He kept apologizing until his co-worker told him in the car on the way back that the only bother was that he wasn't accepting the help that everyone was giving him.

This experience was a huge wake-up call for Jon, who grew up both abused and neglected, and who frequently had gone to school with bruises or high fevers because of his parents' insistence that he was "faking it to try to get out of being disciplined," aka beaten up again. Later that year, he finally sought medical care for persistent sinus problems, having started to get the idea that it was okay for him to get help for what ailed him. After his physician took x-rays, he learned that his sinuses were a mass of badly healed broken bones.

When the doctor asked him if he'd been in an accident, he said, sarcastically, "No, I was the accident." He then told her, revealing this for the first time in his life, how he had been beaten repeatedly as a child by parents who had been forced into marrying when they became pregnant with him. Another wake-up call; the pain of those broken bones had been labeled by his parents as his being a "crybaby who couldn't take his punishment like a man."

Jon had been taught to have no compassion for himself. Like many survivors living under the abusive prime directive, he had learned to consider his own needs, wants, and feelings as permanently so over-the-top and excessive that the only correct response was to feel anger or contempt for himself, and dismiss his feelings as "too much." He had learned to dissociate from the pain of broken bones because there was no place in his childhood where he could scream safely when he was hurt.

Conversely, he had been expected to stay home from school to nurse his mother when she had headaches. He spent days bringing cold washcloths, keeping the room dark and quiet, and barring the door to his younger siblings and father, petting her hands and reassuring her that she would feel better soon. His job in his family was to "make up for" his terrible sin of existing, conveyed to him repeatedly as his having destroyed his parents' lives.

Compassion for others comes easily to many survivors, not simply because of their capacity for empathy, but because their childhood prime directives taught them to focus their care on the needs of others, never themselves. Careful attunement to the needs and feelings of abusive caretakers is a common survival strategy employed by children in crazy and dangerous families. You are likely to be very good at reading people's faces and feelings, and are probably perceived by the people around you as unusually sensitive and attuned. That's because you learned that to do otherwise risked your survival. Your sensitivity to others is a gift, and it came to you at a very high price.

The development of compassion for yourself is thus an essential and perpetual step for an adult survivor to take in her or his life. It's the second truly powerful thing you can do after knowing what you feel, know and think. This is not about being self-pitying (a fear that I've heard countless adult survivors express to me at some point in their therapy), although many adult survivors are more than deserving of our sadness for what was done to them in childhood. Rather, it is about treating your own self, needs and feelings with the respect they deserve. It is about noticing your own pain and distress and taking those as valuable signals about what is happening to your body and psyche, rather than dismissing such feelings as wrong, bad, or overblown. It is noticing without judgment, and noticing with care, the experiences that you have. It is about giving up calling yourself selfish when you are being merely human. It's about having a default assumption that when you're in pain you deserve relief from that pain and care for what is causing it instead of bucking up and bearing down to tolerate it.

Fine, you say, but how can I have compassion for this weak, sniveling, difficult, selfish (you fill in the adjectives here with whichever words got used to beat you up psychically) creature that I am and was. Stop! You're right, but you're also wrong. Children *are* weak, difficult, selfish, fearful, needy, demanding, out-of-control, messy. *All of those things are true about children, and they are just fine, okay, normal things about children*, not descriptions of something wrong. In fact, these are all things that are true to some degree about humans at all stages of our lives. We are wildly, wonderfully, annoyingly imperfect creatures. It is simply that if we are adequately socialized we are able, as we grow into adulthood, to contain some of our human messiness in ways that ease our relationships with the rest of the world. In the crazy-house world of abusive child-rearing, the normal messy characteristics of a human child become insults wielded like weapons at the child's vulnerable self. S/he grows into an adult who has a singularly distorted view of self—a view that undermines self-compassion.

To activate any plan of self-care, cultivation of compassion for yourself is a bedrock skill. It will be the hardest good thing that you ever do. There are a number of ways to accomplish this difficult task. Many psychotherapists today have introduced the practice of Mindful Meditation into our treatment strategies because this meditation skill, a variation of Buddhist Vipassana (or Insight) meditation, teaches people the skills for self-compassion. Mindful Meditation teaches you to use your breathing to observe, without judgment or reaction, the phenomena of the world, including yourself. You observe and describe yourself; you do not judge yourself. You need not live in a large city with a community of Buddhist meditation teachers to acquire this skill. The book *Full Catastrophe Living*, by Jon Kabat-Zinn, is an easy-to-use introduction to learning the practice of mindfulness. You'll find other recommendations for learning about mindfulness in the Resources section.

Many people find psychotherapy helpful in becoming more compassionate with themselves. Several different trauma-specific treatment techniques, such as Eye Movement Desensitization Reprocessing (EMDR), Lifespan Integration, and Prolonged Exposure (PE), to name just a few, can directly address the damaging and distorted internalized abusive prime directives (which psychotherapists call "core beliefs") that interfere with a compassionate relationship with yourself. Links to websites of professional organizations involved in studying the treatment of trauma are included in the Resources section if you need assistance in learning about and getting access to trauma-informed psychotherapy. Be sure that any therapist you pick does know about childhood trauma and maltreatment, and understands what will help your recovery process.

These kinds of formal interventions are not the only ways to self-compassion. Sometimes spirituality or religious faith becomes an avenue toward compassion for self. Kendra, whose father had begun to sexually abuse her when she was three, became born again as a Christian in her late teens. "When I understood that God loved me I realized that nothing my earthly father could do to me was more true than the fact that I was a beloved child of God." By seeing herself as she believed God saw her, she was able to become deeply compassionate for herself and to move out of the crushing self-hate that had plagued her until then. While, in her adult life, she experienced many problems with touch and sexual functioning for which she eventually sought some focused therapy, her view of herself as a loveable person under God's care remained firm, disrupting completely the abusive prime directive of her family.

For other adult survivors, their own experiences as parents have been the wellspring of compassion for self. Nick recounted his epiphany one night while cleaning up after his ill seven-year-old son had thrown up in bed. "I was in the shower with him, holding him and washing him and telling him not to be afraid, that Daddy loved him and he was a good boy, and that I was so sorry that he was sick and hurting, and I had this huge aha of thinking how could anyone be cruel to such a little, sweet, defenseless creature? And then I thought, that was me, and I didn't deserve any less love from my parents than Jake is getting from me." Nick's ability to identify with his son was the beginning of change in his ability to have compassion for himself. Although he struggles with self-compassion from time to time, particularly when he has contact with his abusive stepfather, he has been able to use the image of his own compassionate parenting of his now-grown son to remind himself of how things ought to have been and now can be.

Tracy found compassion for herself in the practice of a martial art. "I went because I wanted to learn self-defense. I thought I was a complete klutz, of course," having been verbally abused with that language through much of her childhood and adolescence by a mother who was graceful and beautiful in her movements, and ugly in her words. "So there I was on the mat muttering imprecations at myself, and my teacher came over and gently said, your critic is not welcome at my dojo. Critic, off the mat." Tracy recalled being confused, running into the dressing room and crying after class, and then realizing that her teacher had not told her to leave. Rather, her teacher had banished her inner critic. "So I had to show up without it if I wanted to learn to defend myself." By being in a context where the pursuit of something she valued greatly required attention to giving up self-criticism, Tracy became increasingly aware of how often her critic accompanied her, and more able to silence it. Practice in leaving the critic off the mat morphed into practice leaving the critic out of the bedroom, the office, and the car. "It still sneaks in when I'm tired or in pain, but I don't listen to it for very long any more."

So however you get to compassion for yourself, start to go there now. Realize that this will be one of the least straightforward and most difficult journeys you've been on. Hiking the Pacific Crest Trail, running a marathon, or summiting a mountain is nothing to learning compassion for yourself. Because you learned self-hatred and self-contempt, your self-compassion muscle is underdeveloped. You will have to intentionally practice compassion for self every day for the rest of your life to strengthen it and keep it supple and active. When you're under stress, which will absolutely be true when you're a caregiver or dealing with end-of-life issues for the abusive elder, you'll have to practice harder. Those are the times when the old prime directives will try to resurface both in you and in the relationship with your abuser. A powerful choice you can make every day is to intentionally engage in a compassionate relationship with yourself.

An abusive elder you are caring for may become angered by your practice of self-compassion. Being compassionate for yourself means that you are breaking the old rules that s/he made for your relationship, and this changed-up reality will be apparent pretty quickly. If s/he is angry at you, that's okay. You can be compassionate with this person without making yourself invisible. Alison told her friends, "I just send her light and love and peace," speaking of the stepmother who had neglected her to the point of ill health when she was little. Remember—*This person can no longer control your life. You have the choice to leave the situation and change your mind. The elder's anger may feel frightening–AND, today, you need no longer be in danger from this person. You have the right to pro-tect yourself, and you need never again be the silent victim of a crime that the abusive elder attempts to commit against you.* Be compassionate with yourself no matter what. In being compassionate for yourself you may also, as did Alison, find compassion for the person who did you harm.

Good Boundaries Make Good Relationships

Boundaries are the places where I end and you begin, emotionally and phys-ically. They are the next set of essential skills for survivors. We are all born boundary-less, having spent the nine months of our gestation firmly a part of the mother who is bearing us, and we spend our first year with only a fuzzy and emerging awareness of the distinctions between those things that are "me" and those that are "not-me." We learn, through our relationships with our initial caregivers, about how to distinguish between ourselves and others, and, in those relationships, we also learn a great deal about who we are. Because I have found it helpful in my work as a therapist to give people information about the processes that affect their abilities to make and form boundaries, I'm going to discuss some of those processes below, beginning with a very quick introduction to Attachment Theory.

Attachment Theory (AT), a large body of research on human develop-ment that emerged in the latter half of the twentieth century, chronicles the ways in which humans learn about relationships and self-concepts. AT says that infants learn how to relate to the world through their interactions and relationships with their caregivers. When caregivers respond appropriately to infants and behave in manners that are good-enough (a concept first named by one of the founding thinkers of AT, Donald Winnicott), infants develop a sense of the world and others in it as safe and themselves as good. Healthy attachment assists in the development of the brain, particularly the orbital pre-frontal cortex where much of our ability to regulate emotion is situated.

Because their caregivers are human and thus imperfect, infants also learn that even the best caregiver will not always meet a need or under-stand a communication. When these missteps and missed communications occur as they inevitably will, the good-enough caregiver repairs the breach in a way that communicates love and care to the infant, places no blame or shame on the infant, and helps along the process of the infant distinguishing between me and not-me.

Many of us have seen (and some of us have been) the adult holding a crying baby, soothingly saying, "I don't know what you want, sweetie. Are you hungry? (offering source of nourishment, then when that does nothing for the distress, sniffing). No, okay not a stinky diaper. Okay, maybe you just need me to hold you. Let's go for a little walk while I sing to you", (drapes baby over shoulder or in baby-carrying device, sings rock-and-roll song slightly off-key to baby).

In such moments when the needs of the infant, while not perfectly or instantly met, are treated with love and respect and reasonably calm attempts to find the source of the baby's distress, the infant learns about boundaries. The caregiver is not me, because my needs are not yet met. The baby also learns an equally important lesson, that these boundaries do not undermine safety or the chance of having needs met. The caregiver is relatively calm (not perfectly!), and continues to explore ways to meet the baby's needs until a resolution is achieved and everyone feels better.

Attachment research tells us that even a child born with an anxious, reactive, or fearful temperament will develop a sense of her or himself and the world as safe and secure when the infant's caretaker is attuned and responsive to the needs of that child. Secure attachment means that the child learns that being apart from the caregiver does not take away safety or connection. A securely attached baby can grow into a toddler who can gleefully explore the world without fearing her caregiver will disappear. I watched one of these toddlers recently while I was out on a walk. Her mom was half a block behind her on the edge of the park, talking with another adult and pushing an infant carriage. Ms. Securely Attached, who appeared to be between the ages of two and three, was heading down into the park with her toy, gleeful. About forty yards out from her mother she turned and yelled, "Mommy, mommy!" A response and a wave from her mother, and the little girl went off in her world of play again.

Infants who are securely attached are more likely than not to grow into adults who have a clear sense of boundaries, knowing that they have their own feelings and needs, and that they are safe in the world, even when those needs and feelings are in conflict with those of others. This is sadly not the experience for most adult survivors.

When an infant is met with other-than-adequate parenting, attachment and boundary development is affected, and the child's sense of self becomes distorted. This has commonly been the early experience of adult survivors. The caretaker who cannot tolerate the normal needs of an infant and responds by withdrawing or withholding affection, or by forcing the child to be silent through intrusive, insensitive engagement, creates infants who themselves can only poorly tolerate connection with others. Self and contact with the other are marked by anxiety and feelings of being cut off, rather than connection and calm, an attachment pattern referred to as Anxious-Avoidant. Adults who treat infants as dangerous threats to their own safety and sense of competency in the world create infants who are fearful of the new, and miserable with the familiar. One's self is contaminated by the sense of being dangerous or bad, which makes connection with others unpleasant and an opportunity for shame, a pattern of attachment known as Anxious-Ambivalent.

Both of these kinds of attachment experiences are common in the lives of adult survivors, and create the foundation for many interpersonal difficulties throughout life. Think of the adult caregiver as a mirror for the infant. If what is reflected to the infant is a picture of being difficult, demanding, frightening, or too much, then that is the self who the infant sees. Such pictures of self, formed before there are words, are then often reinforced in abusive family environments with words and behaviors telling children that they are in fact ugly, mean, or evil.

When very early life has been marked by extremes of abuse, neglect, and other overt maltreatment, infants have the most problematic sort of attachment experiences, leading to an attachment style called Disorganized. Children with disorganized attachment experiences know that the world is completely unpredictable, and that caregivers can be both comforting and terrifying, but that you can never tell when one thing or the other will be true, or for how long one state will persist until the other one appears. The sense of self emerging from the disorganized attachment experience is one of unpredictability. Having a mirror that is repeatedly and unpredictably changing leaves children with no clear sense of who they are. Having a clear sense of self feels as if it directly threatens what little attachment might be available. This is because the boundaries between infant and caretaker remain blurred, as the child needs to over-attune to the parental adult in order to have some modicum of occasional safety.

If a child must constantly change in order to ride the turbulent waves of a highly changeable or unpredictable caregiver, that child cannot ever safely know what s/he feels or wants or knows about anything, even the simplest of things. As one of my clients said, "I thought I liked pink. Then my mother screamed at me, no child of mine could be so crass as to like pink. So then I didn't like pink, because I didn't want Mommy screaming at me and being unhappy. But here's the secret. I think I really do like pink. Maybe. Will you think I'm too girly if I tell you I like pink?"

Attachment and Boundaries

Attachment experiences create what is known as an Internal Working Model. This psychic structure is a non-conscious yet powerful paradigm through which developing humans make sense of themselves in relationships to self and others. You can think of this as the operating system (like Windows or Mac OS or Android) for the child about who s/he is and how to relate to others. As you might imagine, the internal working models of many adult survivors are rife with distortions about their own needs and feelings. Abuse tips the normal relationship between child and parent figure on its head, with the child assigned to soothe and meet the needs of the adult. Having clear boundaries is the last thing possible in such an upside-down world.

So adult survivors, not surprisingly, struggle with boundaries because to have them—to have a clear, felt, and expressed sense of what you feel, what you know, and what you want—feels like a threat to safety throughout life even when the abusive parent is not around. This is profoundly disempowering to a group of people who are already disempowered by the experience of childhood maltreatment.

All of these attachment patterns, which follow us into adult life, can make it very difficult for an adult survivor to navigate relationships, not just the relationship with the abusive elder. Even with a loving, caring friend or partner, many adult survivors constantly fear being precipitously dumped from the relationship. They expect the other people in their adult relationships to have requirements similar to those of the abusive elder, so there is often a pattern of frantic attempts to please which can ultimately become sufficiently off-putting as to lead the end of a relationship. Conflict with someone you care about can feel almost intolerable. Consequently, many adult survivors will either be highly compliant or engage in cut-offs as ways of shutting conflict down in their adult relationships. If there are problems in the relationship, the survivor will place the blame squarely on her or his own head, even when there is powerful evidence to the contrary. You will take yourself out of the picture rather than stick around to hear, once again, what a terrible failure you are as a human being. Chances to disrupt this model of self-in-relationship can be few and far between.

Many adult survivors also unconsciously find relationships in adulthood with partners that mirror the attachment dynamics that existed in their abusive families, even when overt abuse is not present. This is because having relationships where being loved is conditioned on meeting a partner's needs, at the expense of your own, feels right and normal, no matter how much others might see it as exploitative. "Why does s/he put up with her/him?" wonder the friends of an adult survivor. The answer, not infrequently, is that the damage done to boundaries and sense of self by early disrupted attachment patterns renders the adult survivor emotionally trapped in these patterns until the time that s/he is able to analyze them and change internal relationships paradigms.

There also may be biological aspects of an adult survivor's difficulties with having and maintaining boundaries. Lewis, Amini, and Lannon, in a book called *A General Theory of Love*, propose the notion that children with some kind of problematic attachment experiences develop what they call a "limbic resonance" to these disordered dynamics of attachment. This term refers to the limbic system of the brain, the place where emotions are experienced and integrated into thoughts and memories. These writers suggest that our limbic system provides the mechanisms by which infants become attuned to their caregivers. They propose that attunement occurs through a reciprocal process in which each person in a pair transmits information to the other that regulates a variety of neurological and hormonal functions, with the recipient's information then returning through limbic responsivity to regulate the sender's physiology.

Through limbic resonance we become accustomed to certain patterns of arousal, including the arousal patterns created by abusive or neglectful early relationships. When we enter a relationship later in life that has a similar set of dynamics it feels right, even though we can intellectually see that something is very wrong. Lewis and his colleagues write, "A child enveloped in a particular style of relatedness learns its special intricacies and particular rhythms…and arrives at an intuitive knowledge of love that forever evades consciousness." Being involved in a caregiving relationship with an abusive elder may similarly stimulate these limbic resonances to the degree that, although you consciously feel horrible about being in this relationship with that person, your brain is responding as if all is right with the world.

Harville Hendrix, the author many popular books about couple relationships, says something very similar in his Imago theory. He argues that in our most intimate relationships we unconsciously pick people who have characteristics, good and difficult, of the people who raised us, and that our difficulties in intimate relationships arise from how intimacy stimulates old wounds. What's familiar feels right even when it hurts.

There are two very common ways for people to soothe the anxiety created by early problematic attachment experiences. One is to simply cut off contact with the source of the anxiety and try to forget about it. This looks like a boundary, but it's not. Many adult survivors have done just that. They have minimal, and sometimes no, interactions as adults with the family members who did them harm. This does solve the immediate problem of dealing with an abusive person, but does nothing for working through the wounds to self, nor for learning how to create boundaries that include connection. Annaliese and Deb, who we met in the Introduction, both exemplify some aspects of this strategy, as well as the problems inherent in it that can appear when demands for relating to or caretaking of the abusive elder emerge. Cut-offs work fine until they don't. The minute an adult survivor gets back in contact with the abusive elder after a cut-off, all of the old dynamics are likely to activate as if no time has passed since the last contact.

Sometimes the cut-off is not initiated by the adult survivor, but rather was imposed by the abusive elder. Geri's parents forced her to drop out of school after tenth grade to work in their business and care for younger children. But when a search of her dresser one day found love letters to another girl, they banned her from their home and family. She had little contact with the family after that, aside from occasional phone calls to check in on her younger siblings. So she was surprised, angry, and confused when, in her forties, she answered the phone to hear her mother demanding that she fly back "home" the next week. "You don't have kids," her mother said, "Come back and take care of your father."

Lesbian and gay adolescents are more likely than other children in their own family to be abused in their families of origin, as well as more likely to be banned from their families because of their sexual orientation. After such a family-initiated cut-off, an LGBT adult survivor may be unprepared for that same family to come calling on her or him for care many years later, and then may want to jump at the chance to prove to that family that s/he really and truly is a good human being, not the worthless pervert s/he was labeled as when s/he was ejected. A good deal of anecdotal evidence suggests that LGBT family members are assumed to be more available for hands-on family care because they are child-free, or their relationship with their partner, because usually not a legal marriage in the U.S., is seen by the abusive elder as one that can be easily cast aside in favor of the relationship with an abusive family of origin. If this is you, remember what we've been discussing about self-care and powerful choice; *you do not have to prove anything to anyone.* Once you're in that debate, you've opened the door to the proposition that the people who cut you off for being other-than-straight were right. That's neither accurate nor a means of empowering and caring for yourself.

Another strategy that adult survivors use for psychic survival is called fusion. Rather than distancing yourself from the abuser, you stay as close as possible, making yourself meet as many of the elder's needs as you can, practicing self-abnegation, soothing her or him like crazy, being compliant. Conseula and Jack are both doing variations on this theme. In these cases, there is no pretense of a boundary because the adult survivor has remained in relationship with the abuser and changed few if any of the dynamics.

Even if the overt violations have temporarily ceased, the subtext that connection comes only at the price of utter self-sacrifice has continued to rule the relationship. Because cultural norms for Consuela and many other adult survivors can sound like obligations to fuse, adult survivors need to carefully tease out the difference between what they want, what their culture wants, and what might be harmful to themselves.

Problems with this coping strategy often emerge when the abusive elder's behavior deteriorates into overt abuse again, and the absence of boundaries means that the adult survivor is facing blatant violations of bodily integrity. There is also a painful encounter with the fact that all of the self-sacrifice and being nice has been for naught, which can leave a survivor feeling more powerless than ever.

Issues of culture and gender come into play here for some adult survivors. Ideologies of femininity tell many women that a true woman should have no wants or needs of her own. In some cultural contexts people get messages that they are expected to privilege the wants and needs of elders over those of children. However, even in those contexts there are non-abusive families in which boundaries, and the right to know what you want, need, and feel, are respected to some degree. Abusive adults grab at any and all justifications for their bad behavior, and they will sometimes find those in culture, religion, and gender norms. The Bible does indeed say that parents may kill a disrespectful child. But only in an abusive family would these words be used to justify nearly killing children, then demanding that the battered child be grateful for not having been killed. After all, many of those same families probably ate bacon, which the Bible forbids as abomination. Abusive families pick and choose which rules to apply.

Having Boundaries

So how do you get boundaries if you've never had them? You begin with the most simple, and as we've noted, the most powerful of things—what do I feel, what do I think, what do I want, what do I like? Not, what does this person want me to like, want, and feel–what do *I* want? These are very hard questions. I frequently send clients to the paint store for handfuls of color chips and ask them to sit with those kaleidoscopes of color until they know which ones they really like. Then they get to come back and tell me, a person whose color scheme is utterly visible in my clothing and office décor, why they like those colors, including colors that they can easily intuit that I probably do not like very much.

People leave my office thinking that this will be easy, and come back having struggled for hours with the task, if they were able to do it at all. This is why we start with self-compassion, so that they don't hassle themselves about how hard it was to do this thought experiment. Sometimes they have figured out that they love orange and really hate purple, and then get to navigate telling me (the woman who wears many things dark purple, and no things orange) their truth, which is often excruciating and scary for them. Having no boundaries to an abusive elder has meant years of saying, "I'll have whatever you're having" or "If you like it, I do, too." The tears that come when I respond by saying, "Tell me about orange; I want to know how it delights you, because that way I'll know you better," say volumes about how unusual or even dangerous it was for survivors to know what delighted them.

So start with the simple things: touch, taste, smell, color, sound. Become a researcher studying yourself, doing little experiments, noticing what you like, what you don't, and why you feel the way you feel about the sensory world. Notice—do you feel mad, sad, glad, scared, numb? How can you tell which feeling it is you're feeling? Learn to give it a name. Make a list of feeling words to carry with you and try them on. Notice the sensations in your body, your face, your gut. Breathe deeply into your belly; this may be scary. Breathe again, now ask yourself the questions again. Do the Hokey-Pokey, shake yourself about, breathe again, now ask the questions again. And again, and again, exercising this muscle of self-knowledge.

This exercise in gathering information about yourself is an excellent, albeit challenging, starting point for developing boundaries. Because, as the cliché goes, "there's no accounting for tastes," it's usually a little easier to assert your fondness for the color puce over beige, or the sound of Mahler versus the Grateful Dead, as practice for more challenging boundary statements such as, "I don't like it when you call me stupid. I don't care if it's true or not. I want you to stop saying that to me right now."

As you begin practicing self-compassion, you may realize that as an adult survivor you are likely to find even these very simple assertions of self somewhat or very anxiety provoking. The more important someone is to you, and the more you want to stay connected to that person, the more difficult it may be to tell her or him that you actually have never liked action thrillers and really want to go see a comedy this time. This state of feeling anxiety when asserting a boundary will particularly be true in dealing with the abusive elder and any other family members, as well as with the care systems in which your elder is involved.

It is not unusual for people to have their boundaries challenged by others' intentional or inadvertent use of guilt-or-shame-inducing statements. Guilt and shame are invitations to give up boundaries. While not everyone who evokes these feelings in us is behaving abusively, it is very likely that your abusive family system used guilt and shame induction to keep its children in line and following the crazy prime directive.

"Are you sure you want to have you mother placed in a skilled care facility? She'd be much more likely to get some function back if she could be cared for at home," is what Anneliese heard from the well-intentioned social worker who was dealing with her mother's discharge plans. For Anneliese, who knew that she could not live around her mother, keeping her boundary also meant practicing the next skill of self-care, breaking silence about abuse. "No, I am not willing to bring her into my home, nor will I go into hers. When I was a child she physically abused me repeatedly, and I do not feel safe in her presence, particularly when, as you say, her abilities to control her speech and actions are affected by the stroke. We need to find a different solution for her care needs that does not involve me in any hands-on care."

Similarly, Deb's sisters repeatedly shamed her not fusing with them and adopting their attachment strategy for dealing with their father. Because she had also been raised in the faith that they now used as their rationale for continued tolerance of their father's verbal abuse, she was vulnerable to feeling that even God thought of her as a selfish and bad child, constructs that evoked deep and painful feelings of shame. Seeking help from an interfaith group that served the needs of abuse survivors, she found the framework to tell her sisters, "The God I believe in does not think that honoring our father means accepting his vicious behavior. Nor does that God tell me to dishonor myself. The God I believe in now tells me to love myself and others, but not to hurt myself."

This, in turn, also helped her to have clearer boundaries with her partner who, although supportive of some of Deb's decisions about her father, particularly any limit-setting, was not tolerating some of Deb's other decisions about dealing with her father very well. "I have to figure out for myself how to do this," she told her partner, "and I need to know that you'll respect me, even when what I decide isn't what you'd do."

Having and protecting healthy boundaries means that you can be connected while also being distinct and yourself. Healthy boundaries assert your right to be different without losing attachment. For all family caregivers of elders, and particularly for adult survivors in this role, having healthy boundaries can make the difference between good and bad personal outcomes when becoming a caregiver to an elder.

Learning and practicing healthy boundaries can take outside help. Once again, psychotherapy can be a useful place in which to experience having healthy boundaries in a relationship with someone whose opinion matters to you. Physical activities such as martial arts, push-hands tai chi, dance, or team sports are another useful way to get a sense of boundaries through the experience of controlled physical contact with others where you get to learn where your body ends and that of your playmate begins. Sometimes it can help to practice what you are planning to say to someone via role-playing with a friend or therapist, or writing out the script of the encounter, or composing a letter that you do not intend to send so that you get comfortable with the words.

One somewhat obscure but useful model of psychotherapy called Personal Construct Theory suggests that you create a character who has the attributes that you are seeking to incorporate, and then play the part of that person for a week—you could, for instance, make up a character who is appropriately assertive and play her or him to find out what it's like. Classes in assertion may be empowering to you, offering group support for expressing boundaries. There are also a number of self-help books on this topic, some of which are listed in the Resources section.

Breaking Silence

In the early nineteen eighties when the first round of memoirs written by adult survivors began to appear in my library, the theme of first keeping, and now breaking silence could be seen in many of their titles. This was no surprise. Abuse in families is enabled by silence and secrecy. "Don't tell anyone," says the stepfather who is sexually abusing his stepdaughter. "No one will believe you, and then you'll have to go live with strangers," slurs the intoxicated mother when she finally comes home after a substance-sodden lost weekend. "Don't wash the family's dirty laundry in public," whispers your grandmother as your father is admitted to an inpatient unit after his latest suicide attempt. One adult survivor who I recently spoke with told me that her home "was dark, even on a sunny day, because we kept the blinds closed so that no one could see in."

Real and metaphorical blinds are still commonly drawn around the experience of abused and neglected children in all but the most egregious of circumstances. We read or hear the news stories about children who are murdered by an abusive parent or left to starve by a dangerously neglectful one, but we hear nothing about the daily, not-yet-lethal attacks on children's bodies, psyches, and safety that are happening all around us. Those of us who work with adult survivors, and all survivors themselves, know that there is an invisible world of children in pain everywhere around us. We can see it sometimes—we watch a family interacting and think, there's nothing there I can report to children's services, and yet I know with utter certainty that something bad is happening to children in that family.

Social factors can make survivors even more invisible. Ironically, social class and racial privilege can serve to mask perpetrators, and thus make children more at risk in those homes where a Child Services social worker is far less likely to visit because those homes are mansions behind the walls of gated communities. A friend who is a sexual abuse survivor from an upper-class Caucasian home told me that she used to envy the poor children of color whose abuse cases she would hear about in the news. "No one noticed that there was something wrong in our house because my father had the money to make it all disappear like magic. He even made me disappear," she said, sending her to a boarding school when she began to have behavioral problems upon entering adolescence. "He was a pillar of the community and I was a bad, promiscuous, foul-mouthed kid, so who would have believed me?" Although today an adolescent with those symptoms is more likely to raise suspicions about abuse in the minds of teachers or physicians, my friend's experience was far more common during the growing-up years of adult survivors born before the nineteen-eighties.

Breaking silence about abuse is both simple—as in, you speak the truth– and incredibly difficult—as in, you are likely to face disbelief or even to be attacked. Survivors of childhood sexual abuse faced a concerted and well-financed backlash against their truth in the middle nineties, when the self-titled False Memory movement, founded by people whose adult offspring had accused them of sexual abuse, orchestrated a campaign of silencing that included contemptuous articles about survivors in prestigious media outlets and attacks on therapists and self-help books. The False Memory movement's founders pointed to their upper-middle-class, highly educated status, their families' vacation trips and well-appointed homes and said, "No abuse could have happened here." My friend's father joined that movement, even though she had never forgotten for a moment what he had done to her.

Survivors of emotional and physical abuse and neglect have a different sort of problem than sexual abuse survivors. This is the problem of minimization of the harmfulness of the abuse they suffered. While sexual abuse of a child exists nowhere on a continuum of what constitutes acceptable treatment of children, not all adults believe that it is wrong to use physical force as a form of discipline. Nor do all adults understand that name-calling and raging at children does do harm, contrary to the old children's chant that "names will never hurt me." This problem of failing to identify maltreatment for what it is appears to be particularly true for boys in cultures where masculine ideologies expect them to take physical punishment as proof of manhood.

Neglect can also be difficult to pin down and easy to dismiss. If a child does not appear filthy or starving, neglect can be difficult to see. Children who are rarely taken for medical care, or who are left alone at home too young by parents affected by drugs or psychological problems, or who are simply chronically ignored, all may appear somewhat fine at school. Their responses to their problems may be diagnosed as forms of learning disabilities or attention deficits, both neurological problems, rather than as post-trauma symptoms, further drawing attention away from substandard parental behavior. While good evaluators know to consider the possibility of abuse or neglect in a child being assessed for learning disabilities or ADHD, not all professionals know to inquire.

Thus the line between discipline and abuse, between barely adequate and neglectful, can become easily blurred and difficult to draw for some observers and for many survivors. Adult survivors are frequently self-silencing, telling yourself and others that "it wasn't that bad, really. I learned to fend for myself/have a thick skin/find mentors and resources for myself." However, no adult survivor of my acquaintance has ever agreed that the treatment s/he received is something s/he would find acceptable in the lives of children s/he now cares for—a useful reality test against minimization. If you won't allow this to happen to your kids or nieces and nephews, or as one of my friends said, "I wouldn't treat my dog like I was treated," why would it have been okay that it happened to you? It wasn't okay.

Why break the silence? Why, as Consuela asked her friends, should she bring shame on her stepfather and mother now that they're old? There are several good reasons for truth-telling, especially telling truth to yourself.

First, to practice self-care and apply self-compassion, it is helpful for the adult survivor to tell her or himself the truth about what happened, and to appreciate just how large, and how bad it was for the child you were. Telling the truth to yourself that yes, you were the victim of abuse or neglect and that your reactions make sense, makes it more possible for you to then consider how, and if, you want to enter a caregiver role with the elder who abused you. *You are not being lazy or mean or selfish. This elder who is now seeking your care harmed you, directly or negligently, and left you with a legacy of psychological and health problems.*

After all, we do not ask people who have been beaten or raped or starved or repeatedly screamed at by strangers to take those people into their homes when they become old or ill. In fact, in many instances we encourage victims of physical or sexual assault or hate crimes to take out lifetime restraining orders, and to obtain compensation from the state to assist in receiving treatment for the injuries done to them. Why, one must wonder, should the victims of these kinds of crimes be silent and remain available to care for the criminals in question simply because the victim has had the bad fortune to be a child in the family of the criminal, who is one of the adults tasked with raising them?

Strong language, you may say. Truthful language, I say, which is why I'm employing it here to make my point. *Sexual abuse of a child is a crime. Physical abuse of a child is a crime. Verbal and psychological abuse and neglect of children are crimes.* These are the crimes for which the criminals are least likely to be ever prosecuted. They are pretty much the only crimes where the victims will be pressured to forgive and reconcile and remain in contact with the criminal. All of this is simply because these are crimes of adult family members against vulnerable children in those same families. If your elder beat up a neighbor kid that person would have been arrested. When that same elder beat you up you got pressure to not have him arrested.

Telling yourself the truth–that a crime was committed against you, sometimes repeatedly—may assist you in knowing and keeping your boundaries, and in having compassion for yourself. If you're not sure that you were the victim of a crime, ask yourself how you'd feel about someone treating a child you love in the ways you were treated. If your response is that you'd call Children's Services or law enforcement, pay attention to your wisdom! It's not just that your mom was a drunk. It's that when she was drunk she abused and neglected you. *And no, you didn't deserve it. No one deserves to be abused or neglected, period.* Telling the truth to yourself is a powerful thing that you can do for yourself. It is not turning yourself into a victim, as the False Memory movement claimed. It's telling the truth that you *were* a victim in your childhood so that you can empower yourself to heal and thrive, to never be a victim again.

But what about breaking silence and secrecy with others outside the circle of abuse? This is, of course, more complicated. Marty, who we met in the Introduction, had kept the truth of his father's crimes from his mother, believing that she never knew what had happened to him. He did not want to disrupt her view of her husband at the end of his life, and made the assumption that to tell her anything approaching the truth of the matter would devastate her. Like many adult survivors, his boundaries with his mother were poorly developed because he had been entirely dependent on her for what little emotional care he received in his childhood.

Because his wife was so worried about his PTSD symptoms, she convinced him to meet with a therapist who helped him to explore his beliefs about his relationship with his mother. He was quickly able to see that he was still responding to her as the abused child he had once been. "I don't need her to feel okay for me to feel safe. I don't want her to feel pain. And I don't want to subject myself to my father violating me physically anymore. It does him no good, it makes my PTSD flare up, and it's making life harder for the person who does love me pretty unconditionally, my wife."

He also realized that he had choices about how to protect himself from his father that did not require cut-offs or utter silence. He decided to approach the director of nursing at the dementia care facility where his father lived and disclose the history of sexual abuse. "I asked that I be able to have a staff member present when I visited who would be responsible for intervening and protecting me should my father act out again. She was grateful for my telling her the truth, in part because he was also acting out with some of the younger male staff, and she hadn't had any way of knowing that these were behaviors that had predated the dementia. It was so different. I could tell the truth to someone who wanted to help me, and I could stop being the one responsible for protecting myself from my father. And I didn't make myself crazy telling the truth to someone who I didn't think had ever wanted to know it. My mom will never know from me, even though I'm still sure that somewhere inside she must have known."

Marty realized that his boundary, what he wanted for self-care today, was simple. He did not want his father to grope him ever again. He could have that boundary without doing a cut-off. He could also have a boundary around who he told his story to, and expect respect for his decision not to break silence to his mother. Marty figured out that the powerful thing he could do was to protect himself, and that he would no longer give his mother, who had never been protective of him, the power to decide if he got protection.

Some survivors will make the choice to break silence and secrecy with more members of their families or extended communities. Rica's father had sexually abused her. When she learned that her nephew, who was the relative geographically closest, intended to move her father into his home in a few weeks to recuperate from surgery, she became extremely agitated. "Arlo's got a little girl who's going to be three, which is how old I was when my father started in on me," she told her minister. "This is the first little girl he's been able to get his hands on since I left home. I have to do something." Her minister spent time praying and counseling with her, helping Rica to frame her communication to her nephew in terms that were compassionate with herself, and that would empower her to protect another vulnerable child. He also asked her to meditate on the question, "What do you wish someone would have done for you if they had known what was about to happen to you?" This question empowered Rica to know that the powerful thing she needed to do was protect a child.

Rica flew to her hometown the next weekend, after telling her nephew and his wife in a phone call that she had something very important to share with them, and that she wanted to do so in person. When she arrived, she let them know what her father had done, "Not to chase him out of your home, Arlo, but to make certain that you protect Maddy and never, ever leave her alone with him." Her nephew and niece initially had difficulty absorbing what she was telling them, but quickly realized how much of a risk she had taken to protect their daughter from possible harm.

Rica then asked her nephew to accompany her to her father's apartment, where he still lived on his own. There, she told her father that she had "blown the whistle" on him, and that she wanted him to know that Maddy was going to be kept safe. "Come on, it was no big deal to you. Who's been filling your head full of nonsense?" was his response, which put to rest any of Arlo's remaining doubts about what Rica had said. With her minister's assistance she had located a counselor in her hometown whose name she gave to Arlo, "just in case you need to talk about your feelings about this all." In the next few months Rica and Arlo spoke on the phone several times weekly; "I think I'm closer than ever to my family because I finally told the truth."

Not everyone experiences good outcomes from truth-telling. To suggest otherwise would be to sugarcoat what is often a painful situation. Jordana attempted an intervention with an abusive elder very similar to the one Rica had done, but with very different results. She sent an email out to her generation of her family a month prior to a planned family reunion in which she disclosed that her great-uncle had sexually abused her, and that her great-aunt had known of the abuse and pressured Jordana to keep silence. Jordana had finally decided to speak up because she knew that alcohol would be flowing freely at this party, and that there would be minimal supervision and tracking of the children. This was the combination of factors present when, at a family wedding, Jordana's uncle, drunk and disinhibited, had pushed her into a side room and raped her.

The family's response shocked Jordana, and left her feeling alone and frightened. "How can you say that about that sweet old man?" one of her cousins wrote back, hitting the "reply-all" button. "What's wrong with you?" "Oh, Jordie's always been a drama queen," wrote another cousin.

After several days of this sort of dismissive response from her family, Jordana set a boundary for herself and stopped reading the email thread. She realized that in telling the truth to her family she had exposed the fabric of silencing and disempowerment that had not only enabled her being raped, but also served to keep anyone else with concerns under wraps. She got the clear message that her experience was not welcome. She empowered herself to get out of the middle of the Jordana-bashing emails, and figure out what she needed to do next. Her grief at not being able to protect her much younger cousins was profound. "But maybe, now that he knows that he's been exposed, he won't take the risk to do it again." Jordana empowered herself to feel less helpless and invisible. The reactions she received did not negate the fact that she had finally unfrozen herself from her position of cringing fear. Her relationship with her extended family did not become closer, but her relationship to herself became stronger.

Deciding *how* to tell truth is complex. Not telling the truth to yourself is not an option, and the fact that you've picked up this book tells me that you've told some truths to yourself, or to someone who loves you enough to give you this book to read. How and if you tell truths to others is about your boundaries—what do you know, feel, think, want? What are your unique personal and cultural circumstances, and how do those assist you in deciding what will be the most powerful step for you to take? What do you want to keep private? Privacy is, after all, not the same as secrecy. Privacy is a choice to keep some information about you shared with only chosen people. Privacy boundaries are so commonly violated in abusive families that many survivors have difficulty knowing the difference.

What is powerful for your sibling who was abused by the same elder will not necessarily be your path. What is powerful for your cousin who was not abused by the same elder will not be your path. Take the time, and get the support that you need, to know how you will accomplish this act of self-care. Having clarity of boundaries and acting in ways that strengthen those boundaries is worth the effort you will have to exert.

There are a number of excellent general books for adult survivors of different kinds of childhood abuse and neglect that you may find helpful in framing your strategies for truth-telling. That list can be found in the Resources section.

Staying Out of Reruns

One of the most effective and powerful self-care strategies available to adult survivors in every aspect of life is sidestepping trauma reenactments. A reenactment can best be understood as the replay of old familiar patterns of abusive interactions, in which the roles of victim, perpetrator, rescuer, or bystander become reinstated in the dynamics of today's life, even though the original parties and contexts are not necessarily present. These four ways of being are the most common ones found in abusive relationships. Even when there are only two people involved, they can cycle through all four roles with one another. Reenactments can also occur with some or all of the original players, as well.

So, for example, the man who was emotionally abused by his father finds himself working jobs where his bosses are bullies. The woman who was sexually abused picks partners who end up being unfaithful to her. Trauma reenactments occur without conscious knowledge or intention on the part of the survivor. They are evidence of those limbic resonances within the brain we discussed earlier in this book. Both consciousness and mindfulness are necessary in order to detect them early enough to step out of the soap opera. Think of reenactments as a runaway truck heading in your direction. You may feel frozen in place, unable to avoid the truck. You may feel that you have to sacrifice yourself to stop the truck. But neither of these are what you need to do. Your job is to learn to step out of its way and be safe.

Reenactments also feel right in a strange way. This is because they are familiar ways of relating and being related to. When you hear yourself thinking, "Here we go again," or, "This feels familiar", you're signaling the presence of a reenactment to yourself. "I know how this will end," is another common refrain. You think you know the outcome, not because of being prescient. It's because you're back in trauma-driven interpersonal patterns and limbic resonances. You're feeling the hopelessness about the future that trauma exposure bestows on its victims. This is the symptom of PTSD called "sense of a foreshortened future," the one that makes bad outcomes feel as if they are inevitable.

Bad outcomes are not inevitable. They are especially not inevitable in your interactions with your problematic elder. While it may not feel true that you have choices, let me invite you to consider that not only do you have choices, but that it will be better for everyone when you act from choice, rather than from a feeling of doomed compulsion. The next powerful thing that you can do is hold onto the belief that you have choices somewhere, even if you don't know what they are yet.

We've already set the stage for staying out of reenactments, or getting out of them if you've been drawn into one, with our discussions of self-care, compassion, and boundaries. Compassion for self, boundaries, and truth-telling are all tools in noticing reenactments. Practicing these skills will help you to notice the warning signs of being in a reenactment. Some of those warning signs include:

1. You feel trapped, like there's no way out.
2. You start considering suicide as a solution to your situation, and think it would be nice if you got hit by a car.
3. Your health is deteriorating, or you are tired all the time with no organic cause.
4. You feel like your situation is a no-win one.
5. Your boundaries are being routinely violated.
6. You have lost your sense of meaning in life.
7. Your have become distanced or isolated from your support systems.
8. You have relapsed into prior self-destructive behaviors (for example, smoking, drinking, over-work), or have begun new self-destructive behaviors.
9. You try to escape into fantasy (endless video games, TV).
10. You feel numb.
11. You're doing less or none of your healthy self-care activities.

Many of these warning signs of reenactment are not unique to reenactments. For example, psychotherapists working with adult survivors often struggle with what is called Vicarious Traumatization (VT), which very much looks and feels like a trauma reenactment. The authors who first conceptualized VT have suggested that even when it is not the therapist's own trauma being reenacted, VT can reflect the therapist's entanglement in trauma reenactments with their own clients.

Some of these are also feelings experienced by many family caregivers from good-enough families. Recall that a majority of family caregivers endorse feelings of depression or anxiety, and that many develop chronic health problems of their own while serving in a caregiving role. One of the distinct advantages of being an adult survivor who chooses to participate in family caregiving is that, if you are practicing self-care in your healing and recovery process from trauma, you already have an awareness of your emotional risk. You may be better positioned than the family caregiver with no history of abuse to pay attention to your own welfare and take steps to care for yourself. One powerful thing you can do is appreciate the clarity of vision that you may have achieved as an adult survivor. In appreciating yourself you'll be stepping out of the reenactment that's trying to deflect you from self-care and compassion.

Being attentive to the possibility that you have entered a trauma reenactment with the abusive elder is thus a final, and continuing, aspect of self-care for the adult survivor in a caregiving role. Sometimes this is easy to spot. The person who verbally abused you when you were five is doing it to you at fifty. The person who beat and threatened you at twelve is behaving aggressively and making threats of violence when you are forty. The person who got drunk and nearly drove you all off the road when you were a kid in the passenger seat is drinking a lot again.

Usually the signs of the reenactment are more subtle than that. The elder who sexually abused you may start a reenactment by attempting to engage you in talking about sex, or asking you intrusive questions about your sex life. He might make comments about how great you look in a particular outfit that leave you feeling as if slime has been dumped down your back, or "accidentally" brush a hand against your breasts—and you will find yourself minimizing, making excuses, telling yourself, "Oh come on, it's not like he's raping you."

There's the reenactment happening, right there. He's violating you, you're being drawn into the trance of abuse. Your boundaries, your right to your body, your feelings, your safety, are being violated just as surely as if he were raping you. It doesn't have to be ten on the ten-point scale of awful for it to be a violation and a reenactment. One or two is a high enough level of awful.

Gavin DeBecker, in his brilliant book *The Gift of Fear*, reminds us repeatedly that if something feels scary or disgusting we should credit the gift of that message from ourselves and pay attention. DeBecker is an adult survivor of an extremely violent childhood, some of which he describes in his book. He has transformed the skills that allowed him to survive his childhood into wisdom about how all of us can be safer, becoming one of the world's premier threat assessment consultants. ***When your interactions with the abusive elder feel wrong, bad, scary, slimy to you, then accept the gift that your insides are giving you, and pay attention.*** Change the interaction immediately—refuse to participate. Step away from the truck that is bearing down on you, and do it now.

So what do you say or do to get out of the reenactment? You set a clear, firm boundary, and assert it as often as you need. "Dad, I need you to stop talking about sex around me right now." If he escalates and tells you that you're a prude or making too big a deal out of something harmless, persist. "You can have your opinion about me. I need you to stop talking about sex around me right now. I can choose to leave if you choose not to respect my boundary." If he persists, you call the backup caregiver and leave. You have that person interviewed and on speed dial well before you get to this point. Then you get help from your support people, whoever they are, to decide how or if you want to continue participating as a family caregiver. You revisit the decision-making process from the previous chapter, remembering that you always retain the right to change your mind. One powerful thing that you can do is accept the gift of fear, and let its wisdom guide you out of a reenactment.

Living Well Is the Only Revenge

The worst possible kind of reenactment occurs when the adult survivor becomes abusive to the abusive elder for whom they are a family caregiver. For your own well-being, it is essential that you do everything in your power to not go down this road. It is quite likely that you will feel tempted at times to hurt this person, particularly if you are involved in more hands-on continuing care for the abusive elder. If she or he is once again violating your boundaries it's hard to step off the line of attack.

It's perfectly normal and common to have such thoughts and feelings. Many caregivers who have no history of abuse by the elder become frustrated and overwhelmed, and behave badly in the absence of good support or self-care. Don't rationalize to yourself that you're helping an elder to be comfortable as you up the dose of pain meds in the IV to a level that may be fatal. Resist the urge to seek repayment for the harm done to you by manipulating the elder's funds over which you have control. Yes, you deserve recompense for the harm done to you. No, making sure that you get some inheritance even if you aren't left anything in the will does not heal you. Putting yourself further into harm's way by risking felony charges will not close the circle and create justice. It will, in an indirect way, allow the person who harmed you once to keep harming you again, and harming you worse, by drawing you into a perpetrator role in a reenactment.

If you feel yourself being tormented by such thoughts and urges of immediate revenge you are deep in a reenactment. This is an emergency for you. You are unsafe to yourself just as surely as if you were standing on the edge of a cliff getting ready to jump. Be compassionate with yourself for your thoughts and urges, knowing that they are remarkably normal thoughts running through the minds of many adult survivors. Then step away from the role of family caregiver as quickly as you can. You need not shame yourself by disclosing, outside of the walls of therapy or pastoral care, details of what your motivation was for needing to leave, given that many people who are not adult survivors might have difficulty empathizing with what you are feeling. You can tell a simple truth—"I realized that I had hit my limit"—and step away from the precipice. Do step away. *If you recognize yourself in this paragraph, put the book down now and start the process of disentangling yourself from this reenactment.* You can always come back to read later. Your safety is important to me. At a certain point in this reenactment you will commit acts that will haunt you, even if you are never caught and prosecuted. So stop now, please, for the sake of the abused kid you were. Protect that kid from becoming the people who harmed her or him. Step away. Do it now, for sake of the child you were, for integrity of the adult you have become.

One final aspect of self-care deserves its own chapter. That's a discussion of all of the excuses that the abusive elder, those around that person, and you, have been making for the elder's behavior. Each of those excuses is the proverbial camel's nose under the edge of the tent—excuses minimize what the abusive elder did to you, minimize how it felt to you, and absolves that person of responsibility, while putting some of it where it has never belonged.

CHAPTER V:

THE DIMINISHED CAPACITY DEFENSE: HOLDING ABUSERS ACCOUNTABLE

In the criminal justice system, it has become commonplace for the accused to offer a defense of some kind of diminished capacity due to psychological conditions present in the perpetrator at the time of the crime. The crime was committed, yes, but the criminal should be forgiven, or at least given a lesser sentence because she or he was not in her or his right mind. From the infamous Twinkie defense offered by Dan White for the cold-blooded murders of George Moscone and Harvey Milk, to arguments that heavy metal rock music caused an adolescent boy to commit murder, to the assertion that one's military service created traumatic stress that led to robbing the local convenience store, the notion that someone's culpability is diminished by biological, social, or psychological factors impinging on behavior is the stuff of many television plots, and all of the criminal cases in which I've been retained as an expert. Sometimes this defense is true, and leads to a more just outcome, as when a terribly abused woman kills her abuser to defend herself and protect her children. Sometimes it's just an excuse.

Adult survivors are familiar with this kind of diminished capacity pleading, in large part because it has repeatedly been asserted on behalf of the elder who harmed them. This elder did, after all, commit one and sometimes many crimes, from misdemeanors to horrific felonies. Sometimes these rationalizations for the maltreatment of a child came from the mouths of those perpetrating the harms. Other times it was another adult, functioning in the role of passive bystander or enabler, providing the excuses. Not uncommonly it is the adult survivor her or himself who has tried to minimize the horror and inexplicability of what was done by finding a plea of diminished capacity for the perpetrator.

These diminished capacity pleas find new life when the elder family member comes to be in need of care. One of the challenges confronting the survivor caregiver is how to balance the past maltreatment against the present demands. Do I ignore what was done to me and step up to meet the needs of the elder? Do I try to have a conversation with the elder or other family members about our shared history? Can I, in good conscience, refuse to participate? Do I give the elder a pass because of diminished capacity?

As described in the second chapter, it can be helpful to consider a number of factors in making decision about how or whether to participate in caregiving. There are a very few exceptional conditions or situations in which an elder's behavior was truly beyond their control, such as severe brain trauma affecting the capacity for empathy and judgment, neurological or endocrine disorders that disrupted abilities to think clearly, or untreated psychosis or depression. But there are many other situations in which the elder had choices, and took those that harmed a child. While there may have been cultural and social factors limiting the options available to the elder, not everyone in similar circumstances behaved so as to do harm to children. Let's look at some of these variables, with an eye to empowering the adult survivor to make continuing decisions that support self-care when being asked to serve as a caregiver to an abusive elder.

Psychological Disturbance

Effective treatments for psychological problems, particularly psychosis and severe depression, were only beginning to become available during the childhoods of today's Baby Boomers. As a consequence, if your elder suffered from one of these conditions it was likely that the treatments available were incomplete at best and harmful to the suffering person at worst. Inpatient hospitalization, electroconvulsive therapy, and the early anti-psychotic and anti-depressant medications frequently did just enough to return a person to the world, but not enough to support her or his abilities to care for children.

Nonetheless, many adults with these forms of distress struggled to be the best possible caretakers to children, and some succeeded. So why did *your* elder with bipolar disorder or depression or schizophrenia become the one who beat you up, or sexually abused you, or terrorized you with verbal abuse or unpredictability? And what do you do now as that elder, even with twenty-first century drugs and psychotherapies, continues to behave in ways that undermine your sense of safety? How does your understanding of these issues affect your decisions about participation in family caregiving?

There are some clear, and some more ambiguous answers to these questions. The factor that might best help you to understand why your elder seemed to have been not only depressed but also cruel and dangerous, most likely has to do with personality traits and disorders.

It's easy to see that all of us have our own quirks and temperaments. Some of us abhor a mess. Others of us are dramatic and emotionally expressive. Still others tend to be a bit shy and awkward around other people. Some folks are a little self-righteous. Some sing the "me me me" song a little too often. Most modern television sitcoms, and a rather large part of reality TV, are based on the premise that these traits, in medium to small doses, can be funny or entertaining. Turn on "The Office" or "Survivor" or "The Real Housewives" some evening if you're not sure what I mean.

In some individuals these endearing or humorous quirks have metastasized into problematic patterns of behavior that mental health professionals call *personality disorders*. Personality disorders are enduring, persistent forms of emotional and behavioral dysfunction that may or may not cause distress to the people who have them, but which are often sources of distress, and sometimes danger, to the people around them. Think of personality disorders as being on one end of a continuum. On the opposite end is personal style; I'm neat and orderly. In the middle are traits, aspects of style that have become a bit more embedded in who the person is; I can get a little antsy when things aren't neat and orderly. Disorders are at the far end; I will spend hours and hours making sure that everything is neat and orderly, to the point where I rarely complete important tasks because I'm busy making sure that everything on my desk is lined up just so.

The neat, organized, and socially responsible person is the reasonable end of the continuum of Obsessive Compulsive Personality disorder, which is marked by rigidity, self-righteousness, and contempt for other human beings. Expansive charm is what's seductive about the Narcissist, whose view of others has entirely to do with whether they are a mirror reflecting back perfection; anything suggesting simple humanity, and that mirror will be tossed away and deprecated as horribly flawed. Emotional intensity gone awry is the hallmark of Borderline personality, where you become either the rescuer or the persecutor, and where threats of self-harm and suicidal behaviors are common strategies for coping with life's vicissitudes. Personality disorders are not simply quirks, and they are frequently, although not always, present in those who mistreat children.

Personality disorders are also not "how our people are." It is true that each culture values particular personality traits more than others. In some, vivid emotional expression is valued, in others, quiet reserve. Some cultures valorize the warrior or the athlete. Others put scholars or successful businesspeople on pedestals. But as with other styles and traits of personality, people possessing such characteristics behave in ways that are non-harmful to other people. There is no culture in the world that sees harming children or depriving them of basic care and safety as a good thing, since such a culture would cease to flourish. "Our people," whoever they may be, don't believe in child abuse, even when they're the ones doing it. Personality disordered people may use culture (or other personal factors) as their rationale for why they are how they are. But it's simply another excuse.

Many people who suffer from psychological problems such as depression, anxiety, post-traumatic stress, or psychosis do not have personality disorders. Thus even when they are symptomatic, they are often able to place the welfare of children at the head of their list of priorities, and will frequently struggle hard to keep things that way. I have seen this in my own psychotherapy practice, working for many years with parents whose primary motivation is the welfare of their own children even when they can barely get out of bed past the weight of depression and fear. Very depressed, anxious, and traumatized people can be stellar parents.

But personality disordered individuals are often, to some degree or another, impaired in their ability to see other human beings as separate from them, deserving care, respect, or protection. Parenting is a task for which many people with personality disorders are poorly suited under the best of circumstances. It is consequently very likely that your abusive elder with psychological problems had not only depression, PTSD, or one of a host of other kinds of difficulties, but also a disorder of personality that infused those psychological problems with a flavor of rage, disregard, or exploitativeness that was harmful to you.

Compare the experiences of Nathan and Eli, who met because both of their fathers were members of an ethnic social organization, at whose gatherings the two boys frequently saw one another. Both fathers suffered from depression. Eli's father was nonetheless a loving, available parent to his children. He had made it a point each day to remind them of how lucky he was to have been able to see them born. When Eli had difficulties with reading in school, his father would spend long hours tutoring him. Although Eli knew that he had been named after his father's young brother who had died as a child, he could not remember ever being compared or contrasted, except in positive terms: "You're just like my little brother, so amusing and fun to be with. I'm so glad to be reminded of him this way." When Eli's father would be having his predictable bouts of depression, his mother would communicate compassion for her husband's distress, while always shielding her children as much as possible from the worst of the father's difficult times.

Nathan's father, in contrast, was chronically angry and bitter. He would periodically fly into rages and beat Nathan or one of the other children or their mother. Nathan's mother would always make excuses, "You know, your father gets depressed," and she rarely intervened in the verbal and physical abuse. Nathan, like Eli, had been named after a younger sibling of his father's who had died young. Unlike Eli, Nathan suffered during his entire childhood from unflattering comparisons to his dead uncle, portrayed by his father as the perfect child who Nathan could never be. Some days Nathan's father would say to him, "I should have just killed myself, then a worthless idiot like you wouldn't have been born."

Both of these fathers suffered from depression. Only one father was abusive. Only one mother made excuses for her husband's behavior and failed to protect her children. When Nathan was an adult visiting distant relatives he encountered, for the first time, people who had known his father as a child and adolescent. He learned from them that his father's tendencies to cruelty and abusiveness had existed long before any of the life events that the father used as his excuse for his behaviors had ever happened. He also became close to Eli again, as both of them worked at the same small liberal arts college. Hearing Eli's stories of a happy childhood had confused Nathan, who knew that Eli's father also suffered from depression.

Only when he had all of these data was he able to begin to question the diminished capacity defense that had always been given for his father's abusiveness. Nathan's father was personality disordered. His depression took things up a few notches, but even when he was not depressed he was mean-spirited and contemptuous.

Individuals with personality disorders are likely to exhibit dysfunctional behavior patterns whether or not they are feeling anxious, depressed, or fearful. They are the "difficult people" in the titles of the books telling you how to deal with them at work and in relationships. They are the bosses who make you want to quit the job, the partners who are never happy with you no matter what you do, the members of your organization whose presence drives others away from meetings. Many such people lack insight into the destructiveness of their own behavior, even when it leads to serious losses in their lives. Consequently, they have rarely tried to change their behaviors because they are not, in their own minds, the problem—other people are.

Jeff's father was very narcissistic. While he never experienced depression or anxiety, he was utterly self-absorbed, and insistent that everything and everyone around him please him and reflect well on him. Jeff was diagnosed with a mild reading disability when he was in grade school, after which his father would have little or nothing to do with him. "Let the dummy take care of himself," Jeff overheard his father say when his mother attempted to break loose funds to pay for tutoring. "I don't want anyone thinking that some kid of mine can't hack it. Learning disability my ass. The kid's just lazy."

His father's pathological narcissism led him to shame and humiliate Jeff continuously. "I reflected badly on dear old dad, and he took that reflection and stomped on it." What made this even more painful for Jeff was that, until being diagnosed, his father had doted on him and praised his every action, excusing his academic struggles by blaming Jeff's teachers. "I thought he loved me, and then he hated me. It took me until now to understand that none of it was about me, it was all about him."

Personality disorders are stubborn. But some people with these kinds of enduring, dysfunctional behavior patterns do want to change, and can.

They seek psychotherapy, embrace a spiritual path, attempt to find their better selves, because they have come to realize that they are doing terrible harm to others, as well as to themselves, and they are just well enough for that to make a difference. They seek ways to make amends for how they have behaved in the past. Steps four through nine of the Twelve-Step programs are precisely about this kind of healing from persistent ways of being that are destructive to other people. They attend Dialectical Behavior Therapy groups to learn specific skills for treating people with respect. (For more information about DBT, see the Resources section).

People attempting to heal from a personality disorder struggle to be their better selves. Personality disorders are persistent. They are not, however entirely unchangeable. All of us know people who have turned themselves away from these dysfunctional patterns. Perhaps you have yourself taken on this commitment, seeing yourself going down a path in life that too closely resembles the ones taken by the adults who hurt you.

It is not unusual for adult survivors to do with their own problematic traits what their elders did not. As one of my clients said to me, "I looked in the mirror one day and there was my father, and it wasn't pretty. And I thought, if it was as awful being his daughter as I remember, what in the hell am I doing to my own kids? That was the day I started looking for a therapist." Another woman, a personal friend, told the story of how she and her siblings had made an agreement that they would confront one another if they saw one another exhibiting their mother's narcissistic tendencies, no matter how slight. "Damned if two of them didn't sit on me about it around the time I was turning twenty-one—told me that if I didn't shape up now I was going to turn into the same kind of monster as Mommy dearest." This, I learned, was the genesis of her meditation practice, a daily ritual that she had been observing for twenty years when we met. A neighbor, who I had always admired for being a community activist, shared his story of promising himself never to become his father, who had been a fire-and-brimstone preacher in public, and a vicious tormentor of his children in private. "I had to find a way to do good works without becoming everyone's judge, the way he was. There are moments when I have to just bite my tongue. So my joke is that I have a lot of scars on my tongue. But I will not be him."

So does having a personality disorder let an abusive elder off the hook? Not for a moment. Understanding the nature and severity of the elder's psychological problems may assist an adult survivor in making decisions about whether and how to be involved as a family caregiver. Telling yourself, "She's not depressed anymore," may be useful information if you also think, "And she's probably not personality disordered." People can be sober for many years and still be narcissistic, or recovered from PTSD and ridden with obsessive-compulsive contemptuousness.

One final note. While the presence of a co-occurring personality disorder is the most common reason that adults with other kinds of emotional problems behave badly, it is not the only reason. Very severe and untreated psychosis can lead to delusions that the adult should do terrible things to the child. "Command hallucinations," in which psychotic people hear a voice telling them to commit terrible acts are one painful aspect of psychosis. Very severe depression may come with psychotic features. Postpartum psychoses may generate suicidal and homicidal feelings in a new mother. Depressed parents may neglect children out of the deep physical fatigue inherent in the worst forms of this disorder. The chances are better that these parents, if they have finally received the kinds of treatment that are now available and are not also personality disordered, have taken some responsibility for their substandard parenting, and see their psychological problems as a reality, but not an excuse.

Some biological conditions can also lead to changes in personality and behavior that are temporary if treated. Certain endocrine conditions, neurological disorders, even certain kinds of infections, all can lead to episodes of behavior in which the ill person harms others. These conditions are frequently treated and the behaviors remit. Or, if the condition is chronic or progressive, a healthy family takes steps to protect children in the context of an adult whose capacities are affected. In these instances, a plea of diminished capacity is often warranted.

"Terrible Things Happened to Me"

An especially challenging variant of the abusive elder's diminished capacity defense is the true story of her or his own terrible experiences, which were enshrined in the family narrative as the rationale for that person's bad actions toward children. Because abusive treatment of children is an equal opportunity phenomenon, abusive elders include people who have themselves experienced terrible trauma and mistreatment. In communities that have been the target of colonization, which includes nearly every indigenous population on the planet, levels of interpersonal violence are so high in post-colonial eras as to sap the resources of such communities in enduring ways. Many adult survivors also come from communities that have been the targets of genocidal attacks. Other adult survivors are themselves the children of other adult survivors, or of people traumatized in combat.

Given all of that, can abusive elders be held accountable for their actions if they have themselves suffered terrible things? Once again we must examine the notion that being a victim of inhumanity gives anyone a free ticket to a life of passing such inhumanity along to others. The data that we have available would suggest otherwise. Boys who are beaten by their fathers are unlikely to grow up to beat their own children or wives. It is the boys who *witness* that violence, however, and escape it physically untouched, who are the ones more likely to identify with their abusive fathers and pass on their legacies. Sexually abused children rarely go on to sexually violate anyone else. While it is true that a larger percentage of compulsive pedophiles have a history of sexual abuse than can be found in the general population, what is most important is that they represent a miniscule percentage of the total number of adult survivors of childhood sexual abuse, and of sexual abuse perpetrators. *Most abused kids grow up to be non-abusive adults.*

Similarly, if being a target of genocide would create a plausible rationale for being abusive to children, then the rates of such abuse and child maltreatment should be significantly higher in such groups of people as Armenians or Jews or Rwandans. This is not the case. If immigration stress caused child maltreatment, then we should see higher rates of it in immigrant populations. We do not.

Statistics tell us that some forms of systemic social disadvantage do make it harder for adults to behave non-abusively toward children. Colonization is one of these. It is a complex, multi-factorial, system-wide, multi-generational form of trauma that undermines many of the cultural coping and self-care strategies available to members of a colonized group. It is frequently coupled with genocidal attacks, and with aggression against the indigenous group's language, spiritual practices, property rights, and health. In the U.S., American Indian, Native Hawai'ian, Aleut, Alaska Native, Guamanian, Samoan, and Puerto Rican people, among others, have all experienced colonization trauma, and these cultures all struggle with post-colonial depredations, including significantly higher rates of child maltreatment.

This is not, however, an excuse for the maltreatment of children in colonized groups. Rather, it is an invitation to see the problem systemically, rather than as only having to do with individual pathologies of personality. Various indigenous nations in the U.S. and Canada have done systems-wide interventions to stop the cycle of post-colonial trauma and support adults to become protective of their culture's children. If you are an adult survivor from a colonized culture, finding allies who will assist you in holding your particular abusive elders to account, while also offering them the systemic healing opportunities that are becoming more available, is far more powerful than letting them off the hook on the grounds of their own trauma and oppression.

Poverty, particularly chronic poverty, also undermines even good-enough parents at times because it can rob them of their own basic resources for self-care. This said, most parents who are poor are excellent, loving, and non-abusive. Being poor is not, by and of itself, a rationale for falling below the standard of parenting care. One of my friends who grew up in a family that was always strapped financially said that she knew her family had little money, because they had to be careful with spending. But, she commented, her parents knew every single free activity for children and families, and her weekends were always full of visits to museums and plays and concerts. "We were poor in money, and we were rich in culture and love."

The "terrible things" story narrated by an abusive elder to excuse her or his mistreatment of you in your childhood can create complexity in your understanding of what led that person to choose abuse, but should not lead to automatic absolution. Terrible things happen to many people who raise children. Sometimes those terrible things have happened because the elder was willing to literally place her or his own body between that of a child and that of a dangerous person. Helene Cooper's memoir of her girlhood during Liberia's descent into chaos, *The House at Sugar Beach*, is remarkable for many things. The most remarkable and heroic story she tells is her mother's, who allowed herself to be raped by rebel soldiers who invaded their home rather than allow her daughters to be sexually violated. Terrible things happened to Helene Cooper's mother. They did not turn her from a loving parent into someone who did harm to her children, nor did she blame her daughters for being forced by life circumstances to step between them and rapists.

Adult survivors who have been practicing self-care, having compassion for self and developing clarity of boundaries are in the best possible position to respond with a "both–and" stance to the abusive elder who is her/himself a trauma survivor. Yes, the terrible thing was done to you, which you in no way deserved. No, it did not excuse what you did to me, which I also in no way deserved. No, not everyone to whom this terrible thing was done then went on to harm children. Yes, I have compassion for you. No, I do not accept this as an excuse. This both–and stance moves an adult survivor out of the diminished capacity discourse, and into one where s/he can ascertain how or if to participate in caregiving for that elder.

"I Don't Remember"

More than a decade ago I was called by a prosecuting attorney here in Seattle as a forensic expert in a criminal case where a man had committed terrible violence. His defense? "I don't remember. I was there at the door, and the next thing I knew I was being arrested." The expert witness for the defense diagnosed a sudden case of a dissociative disorder. In my own testimony, which came after many hours of talking to the defendant and reviewing records, I opined that I didn't think he was dissociative, based on everything I could find out about his life before the day of his crime. I also told the jury that no one could ever know if he had really forgotten, since there was no way to know if someone truly has no memory for an event, or is simply lying about knowing what happened.

Abusive elders will sometimes offer the same kind of story as did this man, who the jury found guilty, memory or no memory. Is the inability to remember or the claim of such an inability a reason for the adult survivor to put aside your own feelings about what happened and enter into a caregiving relationship, as if the erasure of one person's memory should equal the erasure of knowledge for all? If the elder doesn't remember abusing you, does that mean it didn't happen, or that s/he should be let off the hook?

Our memories are not what they used to be, say all of us as we enter midlife. And this is true, much as we wish otherwise. Processing speed goes down, and our ability to acquire new information and keep it nicely stored where we can find it seems less sharp than it was. We find ourselves in the kitchen wondering why we came there. We go back upstairs, and then think, oh, yeah, the bottle of soap, that's what was in the kitchen. Our ability to acquire new facts, new languages, our latest computer password, all seem a little affected by the passage of time. It turns out that after age thirty most of our brains do slow down a bit.

For those adult survivors who are themselves making the passage into midlife memory changes, it can feel easy to empathize with, or at least give credibility to, someone claiming that they cannot recall the events that are so central to you. The times they came into your bedroom at night, the times they left you bloody and sobbing, the times you climbed on a chair to reach the cereal box to feed yourself and your younger siblings while they were off somewhere doing something more important to them than raising and caring for children, did those things happen if the elder doesn't remember? Does the elder's forgetting change your decisions about how you relate to them, or whether you choose to become a caregiver for them? If the tree of abuse fell in the forest of your life and the tree cannot remember falling, were you really crushed beneath it?

Let's talk about what happens to memory in aging. There are indeed normal, age-related changes to most people's abilities to remember the events of their daily lives. A number of factors are known to account for this in aging adults who do not have dementia, including baseline intellect, medications, health status, and opportunities to engage the brain in new learning. But as many people who live around dementing elders note, people with dementia often have relatively clear recall of the events of earlier years. The cliché that a dementing elder tells and retells stories of certain episodes from earlier years is based in the reality that, even when short-term memory begins to fail, the hallmark of dementia, those episodes stored for the longer term from earlier periods in life appear to persist over time. So the elder should be *more* likely to remember what s/he did forty years ago, not less.

Let's also talk about what happens to memory of adult survivors. Because of the heated debate over delayed recall of childhood trauma that surfaced during the early nineties, much research has looked at the accuracy of adult's memories of their own childhood experiences. The results are instructive.

British psychologist Christopher Brewin and his associates found that parents tend to have less accurate recollections of their now-adult offspring's childhood experiences than did those now-grown children. They compared the narratives of the parents and adult offspring to such contemporaneous materials as doctor's notes or school records. Brewin and his associates found that the adult survivor who remembers that life was hell in her or his family is more likely to have a clear and unbiased picture of the truth than the abusive or bystander adults, who are in turn more likely to put on rose-colored glasses where their own misconduct or inaction is concerned. This kind of self-justification is a well-known social psychological phenomenon. However, this distortion of memory to increase the comfort of an abusive elder can be especially crazy-making for the adult survivor who is attempting to hold on to her or his experiences of reality when called upon to care for that elder.

Jacki Lyden, in *Daughter of the Queen of Sheba*, wrote about her visit to her abusive stepfather toward the end of his life, during which she confronted him about his vicious behavior. His response? "I never did. Never hit anyone. You're wrong." He suddenly shifts direction. "You know, after my heart trouble, there's an awful lot I don't remember." Lyden writes, "I know he remembers. I can feel him remembering all of it, stacking his memories around him like bricks." Tracking the progress of his response from denial to "forgetting" telegraphed to her his desire to be let off the hook. Pleading "I can't remember" is often a way of trying to shrug off responsibility.

Adult survivors also do not always fully recall what was done to them, which complicates your dealings with the elder who claims to not recall abuse. However, survivor's reasons for not remembering abuse, and abusive elders' reasons for not remembering, or claiming not to remember abuse, are quite different. Not knowing or remembering being a victim is frequently a cognitive strategy for staying connected. Denying having committed abuse by claming to have forgotten it can be yet another way that an abusive elder undermines your welfare.

Research by cognitive scientist Jennifer Freyd has demonstrated that the greater an abused child's dependency on the perpetrator of abuse, the more likely that child is to have difficulties consciously knowing and remembering what is being done to them. This model of post-traumatic remembering for adult survivors, called Betrayal Trauma Theory, has allowed psychologists to finally understand some of the mechanisms to lead to delayed recalls of childhood traumatic events such as sexual abuse. Think back to our earlier discussion of attachment, and how children who are abused often experience disorganized attachment in which their sense of self is blurred with that of the caregiver. If such fusion is the only way to stay even a little bit safe in childhood, knowing that a caregiver is abusing you will threaten even that tiny bit of illusory safety. Freyd's research has found that as these individuals become less dependent on the abusive elder they are more likely to be able to know and recall what was done to them. Sometimes, when the abuse has been physical or verbal, and not forgotten, Betrayal Trauma Theory explains how victims can fail to register that what happened to you abusive even though you did not forget it.

This means that sometimes adult survivors have not remembered or identified their abuse as abuse until well into their adulthood, rather than having a continuous memory or understanding of having been harmed. Sometimes entering the role of family caregiver becomes the trigger for remembering or reevaluating the meaning of events never forgotten. One day shortly after his worsening arthritis and impaired mobility had led to a move into her home, Gina was helping her father with going to the toilet. She briefly saw his penis. What she recalls next is, "A daze. I was struck by panic and terror, and felt as if I my body was that of a little child. Then it was like a slide-show started in my mind, terrible things, my father's penis and me, only I was a little girl and he was having sex with me. I threw up on the bathroom floor."

Confused and frightened by her experience, and doubting her sanity, Gina made excuses for not helping her father with toileting, which led to his having several episodes of incontinence. She finally told her eldest daughter, who was growing concerned about her mother's pallor and apparent sleeplessness, but who had been attributing it simply to the added stress of Grandpa being in the house. Andie immediately insisted that her mother see a therapist, and she offered to have her teenage son move in with Gina to take over the bathing and toileting support until Gina could sort out what had happened to her and the family could work out other arrangements for her father's care. "Whatever did or didn't happen, this is doing really bad things to you," Andie told her mother.

Two years later, Gina feels relatively certain that the slideshow in her head that day was the return of memories of real things that happened to her. "It makes sense of so many things in my life," she told her best friend. Her aversion to sexual contact, which had been the death of her marriage to a man with whom she was still good friends, her nausea at certain sights and sounds, her difficulty changing her grandsons' diapers when she had had no trouble doing the same for her daughters, she now understood these experiences. "I got frightened by one penis that hurt me, and all the rest of them scared me, too."

Gina has moved into a care coordination and driving-to-appointments role with her father, and she has backed off from doing any hands-on care, choosing not to confront him. "He was a good parent in a lot of ways, a lot nicer and warmer than my mom. He stopped drinking when I was ten, and I'm pretty sure that all of the abuse happened when he was drunk, because I've kind of figured out that the abuse stopped then, too. He made sure I could go to college, and even paid for me to live in a dorm when we would have saved money with me living at home. I think maybe he knows what he did, and is ashamed of himself, maybe tried to make it up to me. But the point is, I can take care of myself and him too without setting myself up to get triggered again."

Gina did a powerful thing. She did not insist on pushing herself to keep doing things that frightened her, and she did not silence herself by immediately telling herself that she must be making things up. She did not decide immediately what her fearful images meant, or allow others to define them for her. She allowed herself to accept help. She said no to some aspects of family caregiving so that she could decide to say yes to some others, reflecting the complex nature of her relationship with her father.

Finally, there is the reality of the elder who is so severely demented that both recent and long-term memory now is affected. With such elders, implicit, non-verbal memories of being abusive may persist. Remember Marty's father Steve, who began to grab at his genitals again. Such behavioral reenactments do not imply that the elder is able to remember having abused the adult survivor in the way that a non-demented person experiences memory. They are instead likely to offer two other things to a survivor. First, such expressions of implicit non-verbal memory, disinhibited by the destruction of impulse control that occurs during the end stages of dementia, can serve to validate the adult survivor's reality about what was done to them because these impulses are the re-emergence of old behavioral patterns. Because even adult survivors with continuous memories of their abuse frequently doubt the reality of their memories, this kind of acting out by a dementing abusive elder, no matter how frightening, offers an unintended confirmation that what you always knew to be true is true.

Second, and importantly, the presence of such behaviors gives you information about the whether and how questions regarding your involvement in the life of the elder, including your participation in caregiving. The emergence of behaviors that mimic the abuse is likely to change your capacity to be involved in hands-on care. If being exposed to such behavior triggers fear, anxiety, sleeplessness, nightmares, flashbacks, or other post-traumatic symptoms, now is the time to reassess how you will be a caregiver. Stepping back from direct care to case management, financial planning, transportation, or other activities that are less likely to expose you to the elder's traumagenic actions may be a wise choice.

Compassion for self is essential at this juncture. You are not wimping out or giving up, or getting out just when it's getting tough. Protecting your mental health and preventing direct exposure to the traumatic stressor are both important priorities. Recalculating the boundaries of your relationship with that elder is an expression of self-care. The powerful thing you can do is pay attention to what you know and what you feel. *If your mind is flooding you with painful images when you're around your elder, you don't have to wait for corroboration of what happened to protect yourself. You have the right to change your mind at any time about how you relate to the elder.*

Holding Abusive Elders Responsible

Where does this leave you? I want to invite you to hold abusive elders responsible, no matter what manner of diminished capacity they offer in their own defense. This is not to suggest that you be condemnatory. Instead, this is asking you to take seriously that what that person did to you was wrong, no ifs, ands, or buts—and that many similarly situated people faced with the same stresses and challenges made completely different choices about how to relate to and treat the children in their care. Practicing compassion, the emotional position from which you can see the elder as a wounded human being, does not mean making excuses, or minimizing the very real harms done to you by that person's actions.

Elders who have taken responsibility and made amends for their harmful actions toward you may still behave in problematic ways in the present. So be wary of a stance of "I've apologized, so now I'm off the hook." A real amends comes with a real commitment to do better. It's not a wiping of the slate so as to fill it with new forms of maltreatment.

Thus, your decisions about whether to have a relationship or become a family caregiver for the abusive elder needs to occur separate from any of that person's rationales for her or his behaviors, or any of the elder's claims to not recall what s/he did. While this applies to the elder who abused you, it also applies to the elders who stood by and allowed abuse to happen to you when they might have intervened.

Not So Innocent Bystanders

Tanya sits sobbing in the chair across from me. "I am just so angry at him I don't know what to do," she exclaims about her father. "It's like when I was a kid all over again." She had just returned to Seattle from a family gathering where her mother, true to form, had lashed out at her verbally in front of the rest of the group of relatives. "He just sits there, says nothing, does nothing, passively supports her in treating me like that. What's wrong with him? What's wrong with me that I keep thinking that he's a good guy? I think I'm finally getting it, and I don't like it, but what kind of good guy stands by and lets his wife hurt his kids over and over, and makes excuses for her? I want to be able to help him out, because living with her sucks for him, but how can I forgive him for just letting things happen to me my whole life?"

Tanya's story illuminates another aspect of the challenge for adult survivors in the caregiver role. Not all of the problematic elders whose needs for care come to our attention engaged in overtly abusive or dangerous behaviors. Some, like Tanya's father, occupied the role of passive bystander, failing or refusing to intervene when the other adult's behaviors went out of control and harmed us.

The phenomenon of the passive bystander who acts as if unable to intervene is well-known to social psychology. Bystander behaviors happen on the small, intimate ground of families, and on the large field of conflicts between nations and people. In the field of trauma studies there has been a growing emphasis on finding ways to break through the passive trance of bystander-hood so that people will feel empowered to act when they come across someone doing something wrong.

So what do you do, as an adult survivor, about the diminished capacity pleas of bystanders? There are times when other adults' bystander behavior truly has occurred because they are co-victims. "I can kind of forgive my mom for not protecting me from my stepdad," says Penny, "He was beating the crap out of her every night before he came into my room to rape me. I just wish she had figured out how to leave him sooner." Penny's mother's capacities to protect her children from their stepfather were terribly undermined by the abuse she was suffering at precisely the same time. Because she had no funds, and nowhere safe to go in the days before battered women's shelters, her options seemed limited to her.

Kara's mother found herself in a similar situation. Her parents had met and conceived her when her father was serving in the military in Viet Nam. He married her mother and brought them to the U.S. when Kara was an infant. The family lived in a rural area where Kara and her mother were the only people of color for miles around. The nearest Vietnamese community was several states away, and it did not really begin to form until Kara was in her early teens. Kara's mother, Lan, had limited English language skills, PTSD of her own from the war, and little understanding of the legalities of her living in the U.S. or Kara's own residency status.

"So my mom and I had green cards, which I figured out pretty young meant that we could stay here, but I never knew that we had rights. When he would beat her up or beat me up he would threaten to turn us in to Immigration and tell them that I wasn't his kid. This was before DNA, plus, you know, he was my dad and I was a kid and I thought he was going to send us back to somewhere I couldn't remember that I'd ever been." Mother and daughter both kept silent until Kara's middle school PE teacher noticed her bruises and called Children's Services. "And then I was really scared that they would take my mom away, like he had always told us would happen if we turned him in." Kara is able to see her mother's situation as one where she truly had little control or resources.

But some bystanders are like Tanya's father. For the sake of placating a spouse, they turn an unseeing eye to what the other adult is doing to children. Sometimes the motives for bystander behavior are more venal. "He made a lot of money, you know," Pierre said of his mother's third husband, who sexually abused him through his entire adolescence. "I told her after the first time, and she said, 'But honey, surely it can't be that bad. Do like I do, tell him you want him to buy you something. It'll make you both feel better.' Of course I didn't do that, but I lost total respect for her."

Other times bystander behavior reflects a slavish devotion to structures of authority in which following rules is made more important than a child's safety or welfare. Tim recalled, "My mother knew that the priest was up to something. My grades dropped, I was crying, I didn't want to be an altar server anymore. I started to say something and she put her finger over my lips and shushed me. She told me, 'We don't speak that way about Father Chad. Priests are good men.'"

Bystanders are complicit in the abuse of children. Adult survivors are thus faced with an additional set of challenges when relationships with a bystander elder are factored into the family caregiving equation. What may be important to consider here is that bystanders are not necessarily innocent. They are responsible to the survivor in ways that are different from the responsibilities of the abusive elder. Diminished capacity pleas for bystanders may sometimes be appropriate, as for Penny and Kara's mothers. Frequently, though, bystanders have no more excuse for their failures to protect than do abusers for their abuse.

I Sentence You...

Being abused as a child is often a sentence to many years of difficulty. Complex trauma, the pattern of emotional and behavioral difficulties that are a frequent result of repeat exposure to abuse and neglect in childhood, makes life hard on almost every front. Many adult survivors spend years and much money in therapy and other personal change programs trying to simply get their lives to work reasonably well. One woman who worked with me put it bluntly and poignantly. "I envy criminals like my parents," she said, "because if they get caught and convicted, they go to prison. And then they don't have to worry about food or shelter or getting medical care. They have company, they can even get therapy. And it's all free, sort of. I'm out here in the world, supposedly free, hanging on to life by a thread. It's past the statute of limitations, so I can't turn my parents in. I can't get crime victim compensation because it's too long after the crime was committed. I'm disabled by the effects of what they did to me, so I'm living on seven hundred bucks a month. If Medicare didn't cover you I wouldn't have therapy. What's wrong with that picture, Laura?"

This woman's complex trauma picture had been particularly debilitating, and the abuse to which she had been subjected especially horrific. Still, her plaintive words have resonance for many adult survivors. You have survived, sentenced to a life of recovering from the abuse perpetrated on you. When you think about it this way, you might be able to see that your desire, and sometimes your insistence that the elder who harmed you take responsibility and make an amends for her or his actions, is not taking revenge. Your decision to not accept that person's diminished capacity defense for his or her crimes is not being small-minded or unforgiving. It is asking the elder to share the burden s/he placed on your small shoulders, against your will and without your consent, at a time and place in your life when you had no option but to let that burden fall on you.

What About Forgiveness?

"I know that my faith says that I should forgive my uncle. But how can I forgive him? He's gone on with his life as if nothing happened. He feels no responsibility to me, in fact he told me that if I tried to sue him for damages he'd make sure that he'd ruin my life, as if he hadn't already done that. But I should forgive him, right?" Alisha's path to a better life had come through her involvement with a faith community, where she was active in a women's Bible study group. After she had shared her story with that group

THE DIMINISHED CAPACITY DEFENSE

the leader, a member of the clergy team, had admonished her that only by forgiving her uncle would she be truly healed and know God's love.

Many adult survivors struggle with the question of forgiveness, one that is frequently woven into the fabric of their faith. In some faith communities, adult survivors get the message that they must forgive those who have harmed them if they are to be true to the tenets of that religion. Other adult survivors, believers and non-believers alike, think that withholding forgiveness from an abusive elder is morally or psychologically wrong. Adult survivors who opt to not participate in family caregiving may find themselves grappling with this issue, frequently prompted by third parties who encourage the adult survivor to "get over it" or "let it go." Some mental health experts have promoted the idea that a failure to forgive means that an adult survivor stays trapped in a negative relationship with the abuser.

I'm not here to discuss matters of faith, which are highly personal. What I can tell you is that in every faith tradition there will be clergy who insist that you must forgive, and others who say that you need not. In the mental health community you will find as many professionals who think that forgiveness is unnecessary as those who see it as absolutely central to healing.

Let me invite you to consider the model of the Twelve Steps which, as some of you may know, came out of a Christian tradition, the Oxford Groups, as one that abusive elders might find instructive. Participants in Twelve-Step programs get the message that their recovery requires making a "searching and fearless moral inventory," "admitting the nature of our wrongs," and making "direct amends to such people wherever possible, except when to do so would injure them or others." This is similar to the Jewish tradition that, just prior to Yom Kippur, the Day of Atonement, Jews must personally seek forgiveness for their wrongs in the past year from those with whom they have relationships.

When an elder who has harmed you has done the equivalent of these steps—admitted her or his behaviors and made an amends to you, then you might be in a position to consider forgiveness. Forgiveness is not something an adult survivor must offer simply to make an abusive elder feel better. If your elder is approaching the end of life with past bad acts still on her or his conscience, you need not leap-frog over the amends component of the forgiveness process. The elder might benefit from doing that work of making amends for him or herself.

Some adult survivors will find that as they deepen in their understanding of their personal values through a healing process that they are drawn to offering forgiveness to the person who harmed them. This kind of inner-directed desire to forgive, coming from within and reflecting an adult survivor's inner wisdom, is quite a different creature than forgiveness offered out of guilt, shame, or a sense of obligation. If you have the desire to forgive because to do so feels healing you, generates post-traumatic growth, and allows you to have more a sense of personal power, then forgiving your abuser is self-care. Take the time to figure out whether forgiveness represents these positive and healing outcomes before you head in its direction. The Restorative Justice movement has some interesting and valuable material on how to co-create healing and forgiveness between victims and perpetrators of crimes that you might find useful in your deliberations. A link to a website with information about Restorative Justice is listed in the Resources section.

As you engage in the continuous process of evaluating and re-evaluating your participation as a family caregiver to an abusive elder, you will likely do a better job of self-care and maintaining your boundaries when you choose not to accept the diminished capacity plea. Whether or not you overtly request that this person take responsibility for her or his actions, in your own mind you will be in a safer, more powerful place by having rejected the excuses, whatever those might have been. You will be more capable of detecting and exiting reenactments, and more able to remain clear as to your options, including the option to stop participating. Your resilience to inductions of guilt or shame in relationship to the abusive elder and to any family bystanders, will deepen. Your capacity to decide whether to forgive will become solidly rooted in your inner wisdom, and you will behave more powerfully.

Remember—*you are not the one who broke the contract. The abusive elder broke the most basic contract that humans have with children. Non-abusive elders do everything in their power to keep that contract, no matter how psychologically unstable, poor, ill, traumatized, or isolated they are. Nothing you did or didn't do, nothing you were or were not, was ever the excuse for abuse and maltreatment. The contract has already been broken. It is not incumbent on you to keep a broken contract.*

Because so many of the components of how adults break contracts with children have parallels to what adults do to other adults with sexual unfaithfulness, some survivors may find it helpful to consider the advice given to those whose partners have been unfaithful in some way. A list of those readings can be found in the Resources section.

CHAPTER VI :

GOING UNGENTLY

The death of a parent...despite our preparation, indeed, despite our age, dislodges things deep in us, sets off reactions that surprise us and that may cut free memories and feelings that we had thought gone to ground long ago. (Joan Didion, *The Year of Magical Thinking*)

Everyone dies. While some of you reading this book believe that you will meet again in heaven, or that your soul will reincarnate into another body, the earthly reality is that to each life there is finality. Before modern medicine and respirators and the medicalization of the end of life, most people died at home. In the four decades following the publication of Elisabeth Kubler-Ross's *On Death and Dying*, frank discussion about the reality of death has re-entered our industrialized society. While we still tend to use euphemisms ("passed away," "entered eternity", "went home"), we are at least acknowledging that people die. A popular and acclaimed TV series, *Six Feet Under*, was premised entirely around the reality of death, taking place in a funeral home. For the first few seasons each episode would begin with viewers witnessing the death of the person whose body was delivered to the funeral home later in the show.

The death of the person who abused you is a profound and meaningful event in the life of an adult survivor. It is both like, and completely unlike, the experiences had by people whose elders were good-enough. Lyden, in her memoir of being the daughter of a woman with poorly treated bipolar disorder, wrote about hearing news of her mother's death in a car accident. "She was dead, and immediately the thought followed that I wanted her gone. I felt the most sickening sort of relief, entering that gyre of the forbidden. To be rid of her felt like a simultaneous blessing and curse."

While, as it turned out, this death was faked, the story of her demise yet another one of her mother's emotionally abusive and crazy-making behaviors, Lyden's feelings were genuine, and genuinely common for adults raised by crazy, dangerous people. This kind of feeling often has no place to go to be aired. Adult survivors feel ashamed, guilty, and bad about what they feel. The blessing and curse of the death of the abusive elder is a last chapter in the adult survivor's relationship with that person. Like all of the other chapters, it is not a simple story.

"I Wanted To Throw the Ashes Into a Dumpster"

"My guilty secret," said Jason, a mid-fifties Chinese-American man, speaking of the recent death of the father who had humiliated and degraded him since before he could remember, "is that I've been fantasizing about his death for years, like, since I was a little kid. I used to wonder if I could figure out how to cut the brake lines on his car without getting found out. Of course I didn't do it; he always had one of the little kids in the car with him, and I love them, you know, which probably saved his life and oh yeah, kept me out of prison. So what do you do when people tell me they're sorry for my loss? Oh yeah, thanks man, but it was about time? And that I keep going to his grave to make sure he's dead and staying buried? Everyone thinks I'm being such a great filial Chinese son. Well let me tell you, I am making sure that his ghost doesn't rise up and get me. Sounds pretty odd, doesn't it?"

Roni's story is different, but the same. "I didn't want her to die peacefully. I wanted her to suffer like she made me suffer." Her mother had neglected her badly, particularly where health care was concerned. Roni, in her forties, of Irish-American heritage, lives with a number of chronic health problems arising from untreated strep infections from her childhood. Her mother "couldn't be bothered to take us to the doctor. Too busy having fun. But she just had a stroke on that cruise and poof, she was gone. Went from having a high old time to being dead, no suffering. My sister-in-law thinks I should just be happy she's dead, she thinks Alex and I are nuts to be obsessing over how she died. But I can't stop thinking about it, and feeling ripped off. When I got her ashes I thought, shit, I should just throw them into a dumpster, treat her like trash, like she did to me when I was sick. I haven't tossed them yet, but I might."

Ari knows he should be saying Kaddish, the Jewish mourner's prayer. His father sexually abused him and his two younger brothers. "Everyone in schul knows that my father died. He was a big donor, everyone thought he was such a great guy. Did free legal service for the poor, marched for civil rights. No one, not my wife, no one except my brothers know what he did to us. And who would believe it, that such an honored man would engage in such perversion. But I cannot stand up and sanctify the holy name in memory of that man. So I'm lying and telling people that I'm saying Kaddish at a little minyan nearer to my office. The truth is that I will never, ever, say Kaddish for that man. And we decided to ask people to donate in his memory to the legal services program for foster kids—at least that way somebody else who got abused will get some help."

Linda, an African American woman in her early sixties, and a successful higher education administrator, was horrified to learn that she was named the executor of her stepmother's will. "The woman hated me. She put me out of the house when I was twelve, for God's sake, I was on the street thanks to her. If the neighbors hadn't taken pity on me and let me live in the basement I would have had to turn tricks to survive. So now she makes me the one in charge of dealing with her kids, which just pisses them off at me more. They're all deadbeats, so I can see why she didn't pick them, but me? It's like she's tormenting me from the grave. And then I think, well, the law says I can get paid for my work on the estate. But then I think, do I want her money? Except it's my dad's money, and I should get some of that for all the misery she caused me. This is f-ing confusing. Look at me, swearing; even dead she drags me down."

The death of an abusive elder is often a confusing, frightening, relieving, tormenting, sad, happy experience for adult survivors. Such a death does not simply represent the end of that person's life. It also marks an important juncture in the dynamics of the abuse. It heralds other losses, other kinds of grief, opening up long-closed wounds. It can serve as an opportunity for shame, guilt, rage, and fear. Almost everyone who's been maltreated as a child by one of the adults raising them holds a hope, often not consciously known or expressed, that the abuser will one day apologize, make amends, try to make things right. The death of the elder is also the death of that hope, and that second death often opens the door to tremendous confusion and uncertainty, and frequently to more painful and intractable forms of grief.

Elders who were abusive were also often loving, fun, and giving, a source of confusion for the child you were. These deaths are hard to make emotional sense of because that confusion has reentered the foreground of an already difficult emotional experience. Approached mindfully, with compassion for yourself and an understanding of the attachment dynamics that are at the foundation of your relationship with the dead person, this difficult and confusing death can also offer adult survivors the potential for doing important psychological healing work. The powerful thing you can do for yourself at this point is to acknowledge the complexity and confusion of this death, rather than try to prematurely simplify its meaning for you.

What Are We Grieving?

All cultures carry expectations about "appropriate" behavior on the death of an elder. The surviving family is expected to feel sadness, and to participate in some kind of ritual of grieving. Mainstream culture in the U. S. expects that grieving to be brief and contained. Mourning is expected to happen, but within a timeframe and on a schedule that allows the surviving family members to go on with their usual lives, and the wheels of the workplace to continue to grind. Coming from a culture that prescribes a seven-day mourning period for the immediate family I was shocked, when my paternal grandfather died while I was in my first job after college, to learn that the bereavement leave was a three-day affair.

The bereavement patterns and grief experiences of many adult survivors are in conflict with mainstream cultural norms that are insensitive to the realities of death and grief for everyone. Grief is not simple or containable. Rather, as Joan Didion wrote in her powerful memoir of grief, *The Year of Magical Thinking*, "Grief has no distance. Grief comes in waves, paroxysms." Didion's entire book functions to disrupt the notion that grief is easily understood or contained, and tells grief's stark truths. Grief dismantles us. It undoes us. It can take us, for a time, into uncommon experiences, apart from usual realities—we see and speak with our beloved dead, we are haunted by them in our dreams, we sit amidst the mess that they have left, unable to tidy it because, says our magically-thinking grieving mind, to make it neat will mean that this person is truly dead. A human being who is grieving normally will be messily engaged in a normal, disruptive human activity.

Death of an elder in any family, including a good-enough family, also arrives with massive amounts of social, legal and financial complications. If the person has died suddenly, or if no one involved was able to plan for death, survivors must figure out funeral arrangements, write an obituary, decide how to dispose of the body, and what kind of memorial event, if any, to hold. Filing a will for probate, paying final bills, canceling the daily delivery of the paper, dealing with the estate, all of these take time and energy and skills that cannot be developed in advance, as they are useful only for navigating the shoals of life after someone's death. Those left behind are busy with the tasks of tying up the loose ends of a life.

All of that work comes with normal, uncomplicated grief. Didion writes movingly of trying to decide whether and when to give her husband's clothing to charity and realizing that if he has no shoes to come home to then she must acknowledge that he is truly dead. After her beloved father died at the end of several long illnesses, a dear friend spent years having to remember not to call him at times of joy or sorrow. In death of the good-enough elder there is sadness and a hole in the world that seems to go on forever.

There is also the good that lives on after these deaths. The good-enough elder was a source of care and protection. She or he comforted us when we were ill, cheered us on in times of adversity, came to our school plays and applauded even though exhausted from a day at work, proudly attended our graduation from college though they could barely understand English well enough to know what the commencement speaker was saying. The good-enough elder was just that. She or he, a complex human being with faults and imperfections, kept the contract with her or his younger family members to protect and care for them, to do the best to put the needs of vulnerable children above those of adults.

Adult survivors do not have the luxury of this kind of uncomplicated bereavement. Instead, the death of the person who abused you can re-open old wounds, and sometimes creates new ones. There is some of the same grief felt by the survivors of the good-enough elders, because many adult survivors also loved and had some kinds of positive relationships with the elders who harmed them. The experience of grief can also make opportunities available for post-traumatic growth. Sometimes the death of an abusive elder is all of these things.

In my psychotherapy practice I have been taught by my clients that this abuse-created, tangled narrative of how you feel after an abusive elder's death is one of the most mystifying aspects of recovery for adult survivors. It is the component of dealing with the abuse experience that survivors frequently feel to be the most painful and isolating, and that's a surprise, too.

Jason, Roni, Ari, and Linda all have feelings and thoughts in the wake of their abuser's death that feel so outside the pale of usual grief that they fear how they will be received should they tell their truths. It is almost easier to tell people that you were abused as a child than to admit to the complicated feelings you have about the abuser's death. The possibilities for growth and healing in this passage through grief lie in large part with being aware of what is normal for adult survivors and in using this complicated grief to further validate your knowledge of what being abused has meant to you.

The Death of Hope

The thing about the death of abusive elders that has caught the most people off guard has been their discovery that they had been holding out hope for a healing of the relationship. This hope appears to be nearly universal, and it makes perfect sense when placed in the context of abuse of children. Children want to believe that the adults raising them are good, and that anything untoward that happens is their own fault. We seem to do this as children for two reasons. First, children, particularly very young children, are delightfully egocentric. Everything that happens in the world happens because of them. This is what we psychologists call magical thinking, and for the child in the good-enough family, such magical thinking usually operates to give the child a sense of positive power and efficacy that children need at a time in their development when they are actually quite weak, vulnerable, and helpless in many ways. In good-enough families where bad things happen, the adults present usually make a point of helping children to understand that the bad things were not their fault, not caused by anything they did or didn't do, said or didn't say.

Children are, in this regard, very much like the superstitious pigeons of B.F. Skinner's early experiments in behaviorism. Skinner would provide food to the birds on a schedule of intermittent reinforcement—that is, for no particular reason, and at no particular time. What he observed is that the pigeons would begin to repeat whatever behavior they had been doing at the time that the luscious kernels of corn arrived in the tray. The pigeon who was scratching under its wing began to scratch harder, "superstitiously" attributing the arrival of the food to itself and its behaviors rather than to Skinner's decision that now was the time to feed the birds. In the good-enough family, children are encouraged to believe that they can make good things happen up to a certain point, and that bad things are random, or certainly not caused by them, because it is all too easy for children to make misattributions that will be harmful to their well-being. In such families children are also supported through the stage of normal development where they figure out that there are limits to their magical powers, and that there is no tooth fairy, either.

But in families where abuse of children occurs, these attributions about the cause of events get mixed up in terrible ways. Children come to believe that they make bad things happen—but they could also make good things happen, like make the grown-up happy, if they would just do the right thing, whatever that is, which was the wrong thing two hours ago. On those days when the grown-up is happy, or at least not hurting you, you paid attention. "What was I doing?" the abused child thinks. "Hmm, I was drawing her a picture of how pretty she was. Or filling up his drink." Or…the possibilities are endless, and as random as Skinner's dropping corn for his pigeons. Like the pigeon, the child thinks, "Let's do more of that! Maybe if I do enough of that my grown-up caretaker will love me, be nice to me, not violate my body, not get drunk…maybe there's something I can do." Indeed we are problem-solvers, we humans, and solving the problem of living with a difficult adult is high on the list of things that children do when their families are not safe places.

Children consequently do all kinds of painful mental gymnastics to keep alive the hope of being adequately cared-for. Think back to our discussion of Betrayal Trauma Theory a few chapters ago. The theory shows us that children will even make themselves unable to know about or recall some of the abuse they have suffered for many years, so that they can keep on having connection to the abusive parent. Children being removed from abusive parents famously fight their rescuers. Unlike the child welfare authorities, they have not given up hope that their parents will become good-enough.

Abused children grow up hopeful about their abusive adults, twisting this way and that, trying to find the spot in their family's life where they are doing it just right and the grown-ups say, "I'm sorry." and life becomes good. Children who cannot hold on to this kind of hope show damage very early, and act in ways whose result is often that they get some kind of help to get out of their families. Children who have lost hope, whose learned helplessness in the face of abuse leads to severe acting-out, suicidal behavior, or dangerous substance abuse while still very young, are more likely to be noticed by the child welfare system, or by the juvenile justice system, or both. They are the ones more likely to cope with abuse by becoming abusers themselves, the thing that psychologists call "identification with the aggressor."

Ironically, these adult survivors may have apparently better or easier relationships with their abusive elders than some other survivors because they have so thoroughly numbed themselves that they are no longer vulnerable to hurt. And even for those numbed, acting-out, anti-social adult survivors, there is frequently still that tiny bit of hope left that the abusive elder will at last say a heart-felt "I'm sorry" as they exit the planet. The child believes her or himself to be powerful in terrible ways, and is seeking absolution through the elder's amends, which rarely come.

Based on what I've seen in my work, I do not believe that this hope is held consciously. Times when I have mentioned this topic to adult survivors as we are discussing the potential of the abusive elder's death, I usually have first been met with quizzical expressions. Then tears almost always come, because I have brought that hope to the surface, and with it, the pain surrounding the hope. Knowing in advance that there is this little bubble of hope does not seem to protect adult survivors from grieving its death when their abusive elder dies. Knowing about it does help people to feel less crazy and strange and to be prepared for the mixture of apparently contradictory feelings that springs forth when hope dies, too. This hope seems to exist independent of whatever healing work an adult survivor has done. Since so few adult survivors appear to receive the kind of genuine amends from their abusive elder that Kris got from her father, and many have experienced rejection or further blame, as did Jordana, when they have asked that abusive elder for an apology, this lingering hope seems to be more common than not.

I encourage you to honor your little bubble of hope as evidence of your emotional capacities, the proof that you made a fierce commitment to relationship and connection with other humans at times and in places where it would have appeared to have made utter sense to many people to give up. It's the proof of your humanity. I encourage you to cherish this place inside of yourself, the evidence of your decency, of your capacity to see the best self in someone who brought you their worst self, over and over, when what they owed you was better.

I have seen people lash out at their own hope, calling it foolish because it hurts so much to feel it. Please don't do that. As this hope emerges to die along with the elder who abused you, allow yourself to honor it with whatever grief you feel. Treat that grief with gentleness, and give yourself as much time as you can, and if you can, as much time as you need.

"I Killed Her, Didn't I?"

There is a subgroup of adult survivors whose abusive elders died young, sometimes during the survivor's childhood. Ruby's father roared off on his motorcycle one evening when she was nine years old, after beating her and her mother and never came home—drunk, he ran off the road into a tree. Jared's grandfather, who had been sexually abusing him, developed cancer and died when Jared was thirteen. Mark's mother neglected him to get high, and died of an overdose. He was six when found her body in bed. Lisa was twelve when her mother died of kidney failure. Six months later her father began to sexually abuse her.

The death of the parent of a young child is always a painful and sometimes traumatic loss to the child. In good-enough families there are often factors that cushion the blow. Not the least of these is that in good-enough families the children are unlikely to have been spending time on fantasies that their parent might die as a way of comforting themselves. For the child who is being abused or neglected, such fantasies seem, by the report of adult survivors, to be remarkably common. "I used to lie in bed at night and think, if they die, I can be adopted by the Cruz family and be happy," Zoe, a survivor of childhood sexual abuse by her father, and emotional abuse by her mother, told me. "The Cruzes were such great parents. I spent as much time over there as I could. So when my father had his heart attack when I was twelve, I thought, did I kill him? I knew I hadn't, but I thought I had. I couldn't talk about it with anyone, because what if they decided that I had killed him. Then I wouldn't just be a slut, I would be a murderer, too. I made myself stop hanging out at the Cruzes to punish myself. Then I started cutting on myself to punish myself." This manifestation of magical thinking is the other side of the hope equation. If you can control the abusive adult to make them finally be good-enough, you are powerful enough to kill that person as well.

Interestingly, adult survivors whose abusive elder dies after the survivor has reached adulthood also seem to sometimes struggle with this fear that their wishes for the abuser's death have finally been realized. Some adult survivors have rehearsed the death of their abuser so frequently, and in so much detail, that even though their adult self knows that they did nothing to cause this death, a very young and unintegrated place inside the survivor is still operating with the magical-thinking "I am dangerous" belief. I see that belief show up in many places in the lives of adult survivors, not simply in response to the death of the abusive elder who helped to plant that poisonous seed. If as a child you were told "See what you made me do, you bad child," it requires no magical thinking of your own to derive the meaning that you are so powerfully dangerous that you can force an adult twice your size and thirty years your senior to engage in heinous acts.

Here's what seems to be true. Many survivors do wish that they could have killed the elder who abused them. They had that wish as children, and sometimes in adult life. You might have been one of the people struggling with that wish when you became a family caregiver. The death of an abusive elder is not such a terrible thing for you to imagine or wish for. If you're trapped with someone who hurts you and you are powerless to stop that person you might wish or pray for them to die when you are not wishing or praying for your own death.

It's compassion-for-self time again for the adult survivor when you encounter this fantasy of yours. Yes, you wanted that person dead. Death seemed to be the only way you could imagine that that person being gone for good. You were powerless to make that person dead, or even to simply stop what the elder was doing to hurt you or put you in harm's way. It's confusing when you get your wish, because you didn't really want to kill that person—you just wanted to stop hurting, and the elder to stop hurting you. But if you'd been that powerful you would have been able to stop the abuse when it was happening—and no child has that kind of power.

Surviving an Abuser's Suicide

A special field of psychological landmines is sown when your abusive elder commits suicide. Suicide is sometimes an act of despair, a final attempt to solve the problem of unbearable pain in life. It is also frequently an act of hostility, a screw-you, you'll-be-sorry statement to those left behind. Some adult survivors describe having had the abuser threaten them with suicide as a way of obtaining their silence, and some have had an abusive elder follow through on that threat. Neil was sexually abused by his soccer coach from the time he was seven until he was twelve. When he finally disclosed the abuse to his best friend, the friend told his parents, who called the police. The coach was arrested, and after bailing out of jail, went home and killed himself. Neil has suffered from guilt and remorse ever since. "I know I had to tell someone, but I didn't want him to die. I just wanted him to stop." Suicide interacts terribly with a child's magical thinking to generate the potential for extremely self-destructive distortions about who was to blame for the elder's death.

Being a survivor of suicide in any family raises the risk that a child of that family will attempt suicide. Adding a history of parental suicide to your history of abuse raises the stakes even further for you. It is vitally important that you get professional assistance to heal from the suicide of an abusive elder if this has been part of your story, no matter when in your life it happened. Many local crisis lines will have survivors of suicide support groups. Some of these are listed on the Suicide Survivors website in the Resources section. It is never too long after your elder's suicide to join such a group. Living well is the best revenge. Living, period, and not giving the dead hand of an abusive adult who killed him or herself the power to pull you down into death as well is an imperative for a survivor.

There is a large and well-written literature for children dealing with the death of an elder. Although you are now an adult, you may find these books helpful for you, because they speak to the younger places inside of you that are still frozen in the moments where the abuse took place. You can find a link to some of these books in the Resources section.

Complicated Bereavement

Complicated bereavement is the norm for adult survivors no matter how old you are when the abusive elder dies. As there was nothing straightforward or simple about the relationship when that person was alive, so, too, the abusive elder's death is a tangled mess for many survivors. Death of an abusive elder can appear to have many of the aspects of a fresh trauma, and the bereavement process attendant on that death often resembles PTSD.

How Can I Be So Sad?

Grief and sadness about the death of the elder may or may not be present, or they may arrive in a greatly delayed fashion. You may be surprised at how sad you are, and how much you miss a person who also hurt you so much. This sadness may lead some adult survivors to question whether what happened in their childhood was as bad as they had been thinking. How can I miss someone who harmed me that much?

You are experiencing a predictable confusion arising from the reality that while this elder may have failed in her or his capacities to form relationship with you, you spent many years, indeed likely most of your childhood, doing your utmost to sustain relationship with your caregiver. As is true with the persistence of magical thinking about having killed an abusive adult, so, too, the feelings of love for that person may persist. What also remains alive is the continuing presence of the child-that-you-were's internal representations of that hoped-for relationship. As angry or afraid or confused as you might have been at this person, you may have also loved him or her. Ironically, with the elder's death you may have become freer to experience that love, and thus feel more grief.

An elder who was abusive can also have been wonderful, or even simply good, in other ways. Most elders who harm children are not utter monsters. In fact, many of the most emotionally damaging aspects of child abuse arise from the apparently mutually exclusive and seemingly inexplicable presence of decent loving behaviors in an adult who also abuses, violates, humiliates, and degrades a child. "My father was really the better parent," Isaac explained. "My mom was not very interested in kids, but my dad could really get down on the floor and play with me, and he was really interested in me, what I thought, what I did. When he introduced sex into the relationship it seemed almost seamless—we cuddled, so why not this, too? It wasn't until I was in my late teens that I realized how he had corrupted something good. I hated him, but it was hard to keep on hating him, because he was so good to me, too. I think I missed that good daddy who disappeared into the pervert for all of my life."

Adult survivors who feel sadness at the death of the abusive elder may have also had opportunities to do their own healing, or healing of the relationship with the abuser, to the point where the rage and pain are far in the background. If this is true, you will miss what grew in the later stages of the relationship now that this person has died. Some survivors who have done a great deal of prior recovery work have described themselves as surprised to find that there are still matters untouched by that therapy, dynamics that only became emotionally salient at the time of the elder's death.

Death of the Abuser as Trauma

For some survivors the death of an abusive elder is traumatic, so much so that the survivor may experience frightening intrusive images, thoughts, and nightmares. In my experience and that of other therapists whose clients have suffered through a severe post-traumatic grief reaction for an abusive elder, this most often occurs for people whose abuse was extreme, and whose abusive elder was overtly life-threatening, behaving in ways that in other settings would be defined as torture. Often, these adults told their child victims that they would return to haunt them or that the child would/should her/himself die or kill her/himself if anything were to happen to the perpetrator. Children who are victims of the most severe and organized forms of abuse, such as those trafficked for child prostitution and pornography, or those raised in highly controlling closed environments such as cults, are among the adult survivors who are the most vulnerable to experiencing these sorts of frightening feelings after the death of the abusive elder. Adult survivors whose coping strategy for such horrific abuse was the development of Dissociative Identity Disorder (DID) appear to be particularly vulnerable to having severe and personally endangering post-traumatic responses to the abuser's death. But you need not have experienced this degree of abuse or wounding to have strong post-traumatic grief responses to the death of an abuser.

Natalia had barely survived a childhood in which she was passed around a ring of family pedophiles, men and women who traded their children to one another for purposes of sexual abuse. Her parents had told the authorities that they were home-schooling her and her siblings, keeping them isolated from contact with anyone aside from the other families in the pedophile ring. Her father would selectively inflict pain on her and her siblings to ensure their compliance. When she was in her mid-teens she had run away and worked the streets, turning tricks—"At least I got to keep the money my body brought in," she commented to her therapist.

Contracting HIV was ironically her path to safety. The nurse practitioner at the county health clinic sent her to a group for HIV+ women, where she was befriended by the other women and began to have non-abusive relationships for the first time in her life. One of them ran a small business and hired her to work there as a cashier. Natalia finally got off the streets and into a small safe apartment where she lived with a rescue dog who, like her, had survived terrible maltreatment. She had been in therapy for a number of years, and had been doing well, her viral load down to undetectable levels, when she got a phone call from the one sister with whom she had maintained contact. Their father had died. She called her therapist for an emergency session.

"I went into a state of panic," she told her therapist, "and I'm still in that state of panic. I keep hearing a voice in my head telling me that now I have to kill myself, that when he dies we must all die with him." She became unable to work, had scenes of the abuse flashing into her head almost continuously for several weeks, and at one point requested an inpatient hospital stay because she felt so completely unsafe. Natalia's behaviors appeared paranoid to the hospital staff, as she would check and recheck the locks on the doors and windows of the ward, and told staff that she believed that her dead father had somehow tapped the phones and would know how to find and kill her.

After she became less symptomatic, she and her therapist began the work of trying to make sense of her strong reaction to her father's death. They finally arrived at the awareness that for Natalia, her father had been all-powerful, "God-like, really; he controlled every aspect of our lives, including, so he told us, the power of life and death." While as far as anyone could determine her father had never used formal trance induction techniques, her therapist likened the atmosphere in the family to a kind of trance, one in which Natalia and her sisters, one of whom did commit suicide in the year after their father's death, were given post-hypnotic suggestions that they should follow their father into the grave. Her apparently paranoid symptoms were a component of Natalia's inner representation of her father as all-powerful, able to know everything she did, thought, or felt, as well as some parts and pieces of the reality of her childhood. He had actually tapped the phone line into her childhood home; thus, her fear of a phone tap was not delusional, as some of the hospital staff had thought, but a post-traumatic response.

Her therapist also analogized Natalia's situation to that of captives suffering from Stockholm Syndrome, the psychological condition developed by some captives who emotionally align themselves with their captors. Her father and mother held the children captive and dependent upon them for every little thing, and they would offer small indulgences from time to time as rewards for especially compliant behavior. Captives with Stockholm Syndrome become traumatized when they are rescued and their captors captured or killed. This is because the captive's survival has come to feel totally dependent on the safety of the captor. Natalia was traumatized by her father's death, the symbolic equivalent of a rescue, in the ways that captives with Stockholm Syndrome often are.

While this kind of severe post-traumatic reaction to the death of an abusive elder is relatively uncommon, many adult survivors do experience a recurrence of previously dormant post-traumatic symptoms when that abuser dies. This resurgence of PTSD has to do with the death of hope, which frequently leads to a reappraisal of the severity of the maltreatment experienced by the adult survivor. The survivor's understanding of the harms done deepens as the hope of any connection dies. New memories may emerge, or a new perspective on the depth and severity of the abuse may come into focus. Having such a deepened emotional understanding of how bad things were in childhood can lead to a new round of feelings of fear, helplessness, horror, and betrayal, and thus to a new episode of PTSD. This process, known as cognitive reappraisal, is a common one, and it may activate PTSD symptoms for a survivor who understands the elder's actions in a new light in the wake of the elder's death.

Numbing and Minimization

Adult survivors may also find themselves thrust back into a cycle of minimizing and rationalizing the now-dead abusive elder's actions, warding off the anger, rage, and terror that are emerging in the post-death period by downplaying their childhood experiences. *De mortuis nil nisi bonum*, goes the Latin saying—speak only good of the dead. Even those of you who have never heard this phrase may find yourself drawing back from the truth when the abusive elder dies. Writing an obituary or speaking at a memorial service, you may joke about her fondness for liquor, his temper (beating you up), her absent-mindedness (forgetting to feed you for days when you were little). You may notice yourself deploying a variety of numbing techniques that you have used in the past to cope with intolerable emotions. You will try to pass for a normal bereaved person who is simply sad at the death of an elder, because the shame of telling the truth about your complicated and ambivalent feelings may feel too great. Numbing yourself, and minimizing your emotions, are common human strategies for reducing feelings of shame.

Using these coping strategies at the time of an abusive elder's death will likely reflect a particular adult survivor's general style of dealing with distress. If this is you, please allow yourself to have time and space to get out from under the numbing so that you will not have emotional landmines lying around. Numbing is disempowering, and the tactics that humans use to numb themselves are ultimately risky to your physical and emotional well-being. Please re-read the section on Forgiveness in the previous chapter, so that you can ask yourself what a more powerful choice would be. If what you want is to not feel your grief and pain and rage, a powerful choice will not be to suppress those feelings, but rather to find ways to move through them. Like the tooth fairy, death without painful feelings for the living is a myth. Avoidance of emotion simply means that the disowned feeling appears when you least expect it, in forms that you do not choose. You did not choose the painful experiences that generated these feelings. You will be more empowered by choosing the manner and time and place in which you feel them, as difficult as they can be. Prolonged Exposure therapy, a trauma treatment approach in which the survivor goes through the details of her or his painful experience in a highly supportive environment, may be worth considering if you find yourself in a persistent state of numbing and avoidance. Information about finding a trauma-informed therapist can be found in the Resources section.

The risks inherent in numbing coping strategies can be heightened by some of the usual rituals that we practice at times of death. If food was your drug of choice, the custom of bringing food to the home of the bereaved may increase risk for binging. If alcohol was your substance of choice and your culture wakes the dead with drinking, then you need to be attuned to your risk for relapse. Awareness of risk does not require you to absent yourself from these rituals, which may be particularly emotionally important for survivors in some instances. Rather, you owe it to yourself to be mindful of the risks, and get support to keep yourself safe. Leila asked her AA sponsor and two of her best friends from the program to attend all of the pre-and-post-memorial-service activities with her so that she had sober support around her at all times after her abusive grandmother died. George, dealing with the death of the father who had emotionally abused him, asked his friends to only bring food to his home that was safe for him: "No wheat, no sugar, no dairy, please." Jamar, who had been sexually abused by his parish priest, stepped up his attendance at a support group for men with HIV, knowing that he was at risk of going to the bathhouse and having high-risk sex after learning that his perpetrator had killed himself in the aftermath of Jamar's filing a complaint with the archdiocese.

Deathbed Confessions

Beth, who grew up in an upper-middle-class Caucasian family, had had psychological problems for her entire life. She struggled with depression and feeling suicidal most of the time. Sex with her husband was difficult unless she was drunk or stoned, and she avoided letting anyone, even her children, touch her the rest of the time. Despite her depression she worked hard at her job as an accountant, where she was valued by her bosses because she was always willing to take the overtime assignments, sometimes staying at the office late into the night even when it wasn't tax season. Working late was easier for her than confronting her usual battles with insomnia; she didn't think she could remember ever having had a good night's sleep. She also had a number of health problems that mystified her physicians. One told her that she looked like someone who'd been a prisoner of war, as she had scars internally in many of her joints, as well as in and around her genitals and anus. She was mystified by all of this as well, since she recalled her childhood as a pleasant one in a comfortable home. "I could never remember anything happening that would have given me those scars," she kept telling doctors. "Are you sure those are scars?" Often, after a physician attempted to raise the subject of her history, she would leave and never return to that office.

Her father became very ill around the time she was forty, and she flew back to California to see him, as he was not expected to live. Sitting by the side of his hospital bed she received the shock of her life. "Now that I'm dying I have something to discuss with you, Beth. You can't hurt me with it now, and it would probably help you to know. It's pretty clear to me that you've blocked this out, but you were my lover, Beth. You were such a sexy little girl, you wanted it so much, I couldn't turn you down. You were the best." Beth described the next hours as "being in a black hole, down a tunnel, I could not believe what he was telling me. I thought that the medication he was on was making him hallucinate. This simply could not be true."

She returned, dazed, to her father's hospital room the next day and challenged him, asking him why he would say something so terrible to her. "Oh no, sweetie, not terrible. It was a very good thing for us. But every time I've tried to get you to make love to me since you got married you've acted like you had no idea what I was talking about, so I figured that you'd forgotten it all. I didn't want you to forget it after I was gone, it was so important to us. And so many people just don't understand that kind of love between a daddy and his little girl." Her father's crazily distorted perceptions of what he had done by sexually abusing his daughter, as well as his reference to the odd phrase that he had repeated to her many times when they were together during her adulthood, which he "reminded" her during this conversation was "our signal to get alone together," were what finally convinced her that he was telling her a terrible truth about her life.

Such deathbed confessions by an abuser are rare, although common enough that I have encountered these stories several times in my own practice in the last three-plus decades. However, for a survivor to start to remember abuse at or around the time of the death of an abuser is not quite so unusual. For the adult survivor, who had never thought of her/himself as having been abused until just prior to or just after the death of the per-petrator, such knowledge completely and traumatically rewrites the script of her or his life. One minute a person thinks of him or herself as having had a good-enough life and family, and an adult life full of inexplicable but treatment-resistant psychological problems. The next, s/he is thrust into an internal movie that is almost impossible to believe, painful and terrifying, and terrifically isolating as well. While the abusive elder may see him or herself as doing the survivor a favor by discussing the past behaviors, these are toxic gifts indeed, almost as toxic as the original abuse itself.

If you have started to recall abuse at or around the time of an elder's death you may find yourself incredulous, unable to grasp the possibility that such abuse would have happened to you. You likely are questioning why suddenly, at this time of loss and grief, you are having such confound-ing and terrible images of the person who has just died. Even those sur-vivors who have learned about being abused directly from the dying elder have difficulty believing this new knowledge. For those many who have no such direct corroboration of experience, the mourning period for the elder is exponentially complicated by the flood of confusing, frightening, and difficult to believe imagery.

So if this is you, your first steps are to slow yourself down. You may be recalling something true, memories unlocked by the end of the relation-ship with the abuser, as Betrayal Trauma Theory would predict. You may be having some kind of experience other than remembering as you move through your grief. You don't know yet what these images are. Don't rush to try to decide what's true, even though you feel pushed internally to do so and to have a definitive answer to your painful ambiguity. It's important at this point to be especially gentle with yourself, as you have not only lost the person who has died, but you are also now threatened with the loss of your prior personal story of a good-enough life and good-enough elder.

Seek support soon from a psychotherapist who understands the vagaries of post-traumatic memory and delayed recall, and who will neither absolutely confirm, nor attempt to talk you out of, these experiences that feel like new memories to you. A therapist who is wedded to the certainty of either truth or falsehood of what is coming unbidden into your thoughts will do you no favors at this moment in your life, even though you may desperately wish for such certainty. Don't ask to be hypnotized; a knowledgeable therapist will deny that request, knowing that hypnosis will only confuse the picture for you and potentially create beliefs about your life that are unfounded.

Delayed recall of childhood trauma occurs for many reasons, and the various mechanisms that lead to it are not always known, although Betrayal Trauma Theory does an excellent job of describing the attachment dynamics that might lead to such an experience. But the death of the person who abused you is not an unusual cue for remembering. While it is unusual for people to generate such a set of images entirely out of whole cloth, this has been known to happen in very rare instances. It's consequently essential that your therapist take the stance of believing that you are having this experience, not labeling it for you as factually true or false, and supporting you in figuring out what is happening to you. I've referenced a book that I co-authored on this topic in the Resources section. Although it's written for therapists, it can be helpful to you in understanding more about how memories for childhood trauma might emerge in the aftermath of an abuser's death.

For survivors having a first episode of delayed recall of trauma, there are usually several separate rounds of grieving that occur. First, you grieve the death of the elder him or herself. Second, and over time, if you come to believe that you have accurately recalled abuse in the aftermath of his/her death, you will be grieving the loss of your beliefs about yourself and that elder, and making new sense of who you have been. Finally, you may have some of the complex bereavement experiences of adult survivors who had always known, or who remembered long enough before the abusive elder's death.

This kind of delayed recall can also lead to complications in relationships with other members of your family of origin. Len's brother Joey had also been sexually abused by their mother. He had never forgotten the abuse. Joey's life had been turbulent and full of psychological and behavioral difficulties. Len, the favored son, had been less than supportive, never believing Joey's accusations. The conflict between the brothers worsened after Len started to recall the abuse during their mother's final illness, particularly because Len now wanted sympathy from the brother to whom he had offered none. Joey was alternately understanding of Len's pain, and furious at him for needing more emotional care and attention than he had ever offered to Joey when Joey was suffering the most.

Beth, who we met earlier in this chapter, came home after her visit to her father's hospital bed and into her therapist's office where she told him what she had learned. Together they began the process of helping Beth to untangle the meaning of the bomb that her father had dropped on her. In the intervening years she has had a few flashes of what she now knows are memories of her father sexually abusing her, although most of her recollections remain vague, and her recall has never been as detailed as what her father told her. She has been able to link many of her adult life psychological problems to her history of sexual abuse. When she told her primary care physician her story, he was silent for many minutes, and then told her that this new information made sense of her scarring and physical problems. Beth has been able to become more comfortable with touch and sex as her understanding of her difficulties as post-traumatic has grown. She is less workaholic, learning that overwork is a common coping strategy used by abuse survivors to numb themselves and ward off thoughts and feelings of their violation. She still has bouts of depression. "My life makes more sense now," she told her therapist. "It's not a sense that I want, and it's not a life story that I want. But I make sense, and that helps me to live in my life."

All in the Family

Death seems to bring out the worst in some families. Squabbles over inheritance, or over who gets a particular piece of china, accusations that the most involved family caregiver didn't do enough to keep the elder alive, hurt feelings—none of this seems to be unusual. Death disrupts and regresses us. Since even in good-enough families there are sibling rivalries, old hurts, unspoken resentments, the disinhibition of emotions that arrives on the heels of a death can lead to bad behavior. People come to a wake or a shiva, drink too much, and say ugly things. Family secrets are thrust into the light in ways that are reactive rather than thoughtful.

Add a history of child maltreatment to this picture, and realize that for the adult survivor, the death of an abusive elder may also create, or widen, cracks in a shaky family system. Such a death can also cement solidarity among survivor peers. Depending on how well-integrated the truths of your experiences are into the larger family narrative, the death of the abusive elder will create conditions in which your relationship with your family of origin may change, sometimes for better, sometimes for harder.

Even if you know that there are other members of your generation who are also survivors of maltreatment at the hands of the dead person, you cannot expect that your experience of the abuse, or the death, will be anything like your own. Many adult survivors see their co-victims for the first time in many years at events surrounding the death of the abusive elder. Those encounters can make survivors painfully aware that their particular resolution to the abuse is not the one shared by the people who they have long thought of as their comrades in suffering.

Casey's father had paranoid schizophrenia, and even when he was finally medicated he continued to be cruel to his children, depriving the family of food and light because of his delusion that they had no money to pay electrical bills, and screaming imprecations at them any time they would make noise while playing. She and her two younger brothers had scattered across the country, making lives for themselves apart from their parents and one another, having infrequent phone and email contact. Gathered back in St. Louis for his funeral, she attempted to engage her brothers in conversation about what had happened to all of them. "What are you talking about?" said her youngest brother, Roy. "All I can remember is that you were a little brat and annoyed him all the time and got us into trouble." Casey and their other brother, Harley, were shocked at what felt like a crazy distortion of what had happened. "Oh come on, Case, even if what everything you say is true, and maybe it is, so what. He was sick, and that was a long time ago." Roy had become deeply involved in a religious faith in his adulthood, and went on to share his belief that they were called upon to forgive and honor their father, and that was what he intended to do.

Casey realized that she had been carrying a story line of "me and my brothers against the world," one that had comforted her in times of difficulty. She lost a part of her story that day at the funeral. "It's hard to come out as the child of someone with schizophrenia, because most people know it's inherited, and then they'll start looking at me like I'm mentally ill, which I'm not. So I had a club to comfort myself with, me and Roy and Harley, and it turns out Roy's not in the club. It's a little lonelier there in the clubhouse inside my head."

Marla had maintained a close relationship with her parents, who had both been verbally abusive to her and her six siblings. The youngest child in the family, she ensured that she lived in close proximity to them, running errands, bringing them meals, and nursing them both through their final illnesses, all while receiving a large helping of scorn and derision from her older siblings who wanted nothing to do with their parents. Each parent died in relatively quick succession. When the will was read Marla was shocked and horrified to find that she had been cut out of the estate completely, and that the entirety of it had been left to her elder brother, the only son.

"I know I shouldn't have expected that they would leave me something, but I did. I took care of them! I went over to their house after work and cleaned and cooked for them! I put off getting married because I was afraid I wouldn't have enough for my parents. How could they do this?" Marla became unable to grieve for her parents, and was frequently consumed with rage at them. Her sisters were unsympathetic, with variations on the theme of "I told you so" coloring their communications with her. Her relationships with her older siblings, which had already been difficult, became even worse, and she felt completely alone in the world.

It took a very long time for Marla to retrieve meaning and healing from what happened around the death of her parents. Being disinherited opened up the wounds of childhood trauma that she had been covering over by becoming the family caregiver to both abusive parents. Over the course of several years she was able to reach a point of grief for herself for having been so terribly exploited, and a developed an increased awareness of how her inability to know or have boundaries had rendered her vulnerable to that and other interpersonal exploitations in her adult life. She has slowly begun to empower herself to become more in charge of what she does in her life, working hard to give up the notion that things "happen" to her, and instead embracing her abilities to make her life more of what she wants it to be. She has learned to have compassion for herself and the choices she made to sacrifice herself to her family's abusive system.

Her relationships with her siblings have grown slightly less painful, but much more distant, in large part because this is what she wants. She still finds it hard to set limits with them when they ask her, the family's official Cinderella, to do them a favor. She tries not to resent her brother for never offering her any of the money he inherited, only because she knows that his good financial fortune came at a high emotional price. "But then I remind myself that I've never really been loved for being a doormat. All I've ever been is pitied or looked down on." Because it is not unusual for some siblings in a family where all were abused to identify with the abusive elders and develop abusive relationships with sisters or brothers, survivors need to be prepared for a sibling to step into the role of perpetrator—and thus also prepared to have clear boundaries and not enter a reenactment.

Sometimes the adult survivor generation is able to wrest power back from the hands of the elder who has died. Survivors can and sometimes do disrupt the patterns of abuse, pain, and distrust to create stronger and more loving relationships among themselves. Glen sent an email out to his siblings and first cousins when he learned of their grandmother's death, inviting "anyone who has a story about Nana that's been hard to share to get together with me after the service" at a private space he had rented. Glen had been planning for this day for many years. He had discussed with his therapist how he could best use the death of a woman who had been verbally and emotionally abusive to many of them, and had hurt their parents as well, to create an opportunity for healing.

"I was scared no one would show up," he later told his therapist. But show up they did. Both of his brothers, three of his male and one female first cousin gathered at a hotel room in Phoenix. "I told them that I knew that Nana had been cruel to a lot of us, especially the boys, and that this hadn't helped our relationships with each other. And that I was hoping that because now no one had to worry about hurting her feelings and being screamed at anymore that we could actually talk to one another." Tears filled Glen's eyes as he recounted how the family members, slowly, then like a torrent, told their experiences of being the target of a woman with great power and immense rage, from the time of their earliest recollections.

Not every family will have a member who is as intentional as Glen about breaking the silences among a group of adult survivors within a family, and not everyone who does this kind of intervention will achieve the result of greater closeness with their family. In some families where abuse and maltreatment of children has occurred, the wounds to the fabric of the family system are so deep as to defy initial intervention.

Divide and conquer is a common tactic of abusive adults who have targeted more than one child in a family, and it can be difficult for the official winners of the family lottery to admit the price they paid for the favor shown them by an abuser who hurt them less than the other children in the family. When one sibling was abused and others were not some of these dynamics can be especially sticky to deal with. An important piece of being powerful in such a situation is to remember that your sibling was also a child, and also had the choice of bad or worse—and then to know that your now-adult sibling, like the elders who harmed you, has the option as an adult to pull out of the abusive family system rules and heal the relationship with you.

But the death of the abusive elder can be an opportunity. It offers an opening of the family system, a grace period before that system shuts again and re-crystallizes around dynamics that enabled abuse. Only you can assess your capacity and willingness to use this opening to try to create change in your family of origin. Only you know whether you have the inner resources and outer support necessary to weather whatever might happen should you take the risk to empower yourself and others in the family to tell truths and be more healed.

If you're considering having the kind of talk that Glen did with his family peers, no matter how informally, take care of yourself. Talk over your idea and plans well in advance if you can with someone who you trust—a therapist, a clergyperson, a friend—so that you can reason out the pros and cons, and explore what the most likely risks to you will be, both if you try to say something, and also if you do not. That last piece is an important consideration. We are usually quite aware of the risks inherent in taking action. We rarely attend to the risks we have already assumed that we must bear, inherent in our current stance. There are risks in being silent, risks of isolation, invalidation, and disconnection from people who could be sources of great support.

I invite you to weigh the risks of things as they are against the risks of speaking up and out in the wake of an abusive elder's death. You may decide to wait until after a formal memorial service or ritual grieving period is over. Simply because many of the people you want to speak with are likely to be in one physical location does not mean that you, or they, are emotionally ready to speak truths about what happened in childhood. Be deliberate and planful, so that you can take the best care of yourself possible. You know that the elder will die at some future point if she or he has not already; use this time well, on behalf of your healing. This is an opportunity for post-traumatic growth for you as well as your family members, a time for you to get care.

One of the many distorted lessons of abuse is that the abused child does not deserve care or consideration. Don't apply that lesson to this exercise. If you choose to take Glen's direction, do so in a way that respects your unique capacities as well as your vulnerabilities, and that honors what will be most healing. The elder is dead. You're still here. Time is now on your side.

All Alone

For survivors who are only children, or only surviving children, the death of an abusive elder may carry special emotional complications. Zeke was an only child whose mother, the good-enough parent, had died when he was in his early twenties, and he had lost contact with her extended family. His father, who had been workaholic and verbally abusive, lived on the opposite coast, and Zeke had forced himself to visit once every year or so. "The old man doesn't have anyone else in his life," he told his bandmates, who never looked forward to their drummer's absence: "You're gone before you go, and you're not back for weeks after you get home," was how the lead singer described it to him.

His father died after a fall in his bathroom, an angry loner whose body was finally found after the mail carrier notified law enforcement that the mail hadn't been taken in for weeks. Zeke's emotional responses ran the gamut of relief, anger, and sadness. "And then I started to think that I was like him. I was alone in the world. I had the band, so if I died in the bathroom someone would miss me sooner. But that's it. I've kept everyone at a distance." Because Zeke had coped with his feelings of utter worthlessness and inadequacy by avoiding close relationships, he was relatively isolated emotionally. He realized that he had allowed his mother's extended family, who he remembered as kind to him, to become distant out of those feelings of worthlessness.

He had also, he realized, acted from loyalty to his father, who had always derided his mother and her kin as lazy and soft-hearted; "I know now that I kept hoping to get him to see something in me that would make him be good to me. Now that he's dead and I'm not somehow trying to prove to him that I'm not like them, it feels too late to go to them and ask them to allow me back in to the family. But that's what I want. I miss having family."

If this is your story, it may be especially important for you to find additional emotional support during the period surrounding the death of your abusive elder. In finding support, be attentive to ensuring that whoever you welcome into your network of care does not collude with silencing you or minimizing the realities of your early life while you work through your loss. Honesty about the complexities of your bereavement, and the special circumstances that may be present because your childhood pain was unwitnessed, must be central to the understandings shared by you and your support team.

What if you did not grow up as an only child, but are now alone because you have lost siblings to death? Some of the answers to this question lie in the context of your sibling's death. When your sibling's death is part of the aftermath of maltreatment, your choices for how to respond to the elder's death become exponentially more confusing. Nicole's sister Kate had killed herself when they were both in their twenties. Nicole had lived through the subsequent three decades with guilt over having been the one who had been able to survive the psychological consequences of the physical and emotional abuse that they had both suffered as children at the hands of an older half-brother. His death a few years past had been complicated for Nicole, who had not attended the funeral, despite the pleading of her mother, a single parent who had raised Nicole and Kate while turning her head away from the depredations inflicted on her daughters by her son. When her mother died next, Nicole found herself in a painful quandary.

"I should do something for her, arrange a memorial service, something. I'm the only kid left. But what do you say about a woman who let that happen and kept making excuses for him? What do you say about a woman who let her daughter die from that? How do I explain that to the rest of the family?" Nicole realized that her mother had left her one more set of bad choices. Her mother's death also re-opened her grief about her sister's suicide, and her feelings of survivor guilt.

If you, like Nicole, are living with such a set of bad choices, remember that care for yourself is going to be your highest priority. The elder is dead. Take the time you need to decide how you want to respond to that death. Figure out if or how you want to honor the memory of your dead sibling in the process of responding to the death of a difficult elder. Nicole's mother had been neglectful, a bystander who allowed terrible things to happen while turning away as if helpless. Nicole decided that she was at risk of sliding into a trauma reenactment if she remained paralyzed by her indecision. She had to do something on her own behalf, not turn her head away from her own pain and confusion and hope that they would pass by. She asked her mother's youngest sister, to whom she had told the story of the abuse at the time of her half-brother's death, to take over the process of arranging a memorial. "I can't do it for her," she told her aunt. "I need the family to take care of me, and to realize that I'm losing Katie all over again. Because even if she acted like it was no big deal, Mom was the only other person who knew what Danny did to us. The only other one who ever saw it, even though she didn't do a damn thing about it." Nicole identified the importance of having her status as the sole survivor, and her grief as a sister, recognized in the context of her mother's death.

If you are the sole survivor, a component of empowering yourself through this period after the death of an abusive or neglectful elder will thus be to become witnessed. A fascinating body of research on how children remember the events of their early lives tells us that many early memories are consolidated because the child participates in the experiences with someone else, who then reflects the experience back to the child through conversation and shared remembering. "Remember when" is the root of our abilities to know the story line of our lives, what developmental psychologists call "autobiographical memory." When you "alone are left to tell the tale," like the narrator in *Moby Dick*, then like Ishmael, you need to find a listener for your story.

The Root of All Conflict

Many elders who were abusive to children will leave little or nothing by way of money to those who survive them. This is because, as we discussed in an earlier chapter, there are relationships between the psychological problems underlying an adult's maltreatment of children and poor self-care. Gambling and compulsive spending, substance abuse, ill health, and poor judgment may have all conspired to ensure that your elder died in debt, not with money to gift to the heirs. But having money to leave creates other complications. Abusive elders who do have an estate may use a will as a means of continuing to punish and manipulate the next generation. Even when there is no money there are sometimes symbolic items, possessions that convey specific meaning to you that you have hoped you will someday have for your own. An abusive elder can reach from inside the grave to stir the pot among those left behind by ensuring that no one gets what might heal them.

As many as fifty-five percent of all people die without having written a will; the percentages of people who die intestate go up even sharply for African-Americans (sixty-eight percent) and Latino/as (seventy-four percent). Adult survivors who have relationships with their abusive elders are often in awkward positions vis a vis encouraging an elder to write a will. Wills serve an organizing function for the estate of the dead person, and reduce the amount of chaos, confusion, and conflict that may emerge among heirs to an estate, no matter how small. But because of the same psychological and behavioral problems that were the source of the abusive behaviors, abusive elders are often less likely to demonstrate the kinds of planful, thoughtful behavior, and desire to reduce the stress on their heirs, that goes into writing a will. Writing a will is, after all, an act that acknowledges the existential reality that we all die. Elders who could not tolerate caring for children are often also poorly equipped emotionally to confront the reality of their own mortality.

Even when there is no will, an estate must be administered by someone. Adult survivors may also find themselves asked to take on the role of personal representative or executor of the estate of the abusive elder, will or no will, as was true for Linda. The person who performs this role is charged with tying up all financial affairs of the estate, including disbursement of inheritances and settling of debts.

The task of an executor is a very emotionally intimate one because it places you in regular personal contact with the financial and personal dealings of the dead person. One adult survivor of sexual abuse who was executor of his father's estate encountered stacks of child pornography in the house. He described feeling torn between the desire to burn it all, and the thought that he should give the photos to legal authorities in the hopes of helping find and prosecute the people who had made them. Another survivor spoke with me about cleaning out hundreds, perhaps thousands of empty liquor bottles, in addition to scores of still-full ones, from all over her dead mother's house. "I went to a lot of Al-Anon meetings that week," she told me. "Her booze was more important to her than me even after she died, and it took a lot of meditating and praying on it not to have her consume my life while I was cleaning out her stashes."

Each of these adult survivors described intensification of PTSD symptoms during their time as executors of their abusive parents' estates. For Marco, who ultimately turned the pornography over to the police, the retraumatization he experienced from encountering scenes of other children being violated was lessened somewhat by that decision. He told me, "I couldn't put my father in jail for what he did to me, but maybe I'll put someone else there. If I have the chance to stop one other child from suffering then it's worth it."

Being an executor is technically largely administrative and time-consuming, and involves such activities as searching for all assets, liquidating assets as needed, filing for probate if this is required, disbursing inheritances, dealing with Social Security, the Veteran's Administration, banks, credit card companies—in short, becoming the financial alter ego of the person who has died. While it is a paid position, serving in this role for the estate of a person who abused you may be sufficiently painful that no amount of money will be adequate compensation. Linda's ambivalence about taking on that job is common even for people who were not abused.

Because the executor is stepping into the life of the dead person, playing this part can be both disruptive and empowering to the adult survivor. At times, as was true for Linda, this assignment seems onerous. It can feel like one last act of abuse because the executor is in the role of dealing with heirs, some of whom are unhappy with what they have been left, some of whom may be deciding to sue the estate because they believe they have been treated unfairly, and some of whom are angry at the executor for not getting funds to them more quickly. If you have been named as the executor in a will by an abusive elder and you realize that you want to have nothing to do with this job, you can petition the probate court to remove you and appoint someone else.

You can also use estate funds to hire someone else to do some or all of the tasks. Ashley, who had become literally sickened by the task of dealing with her late mother's collection of alcohol bottles, figured out quickly that she needed to stay out the house where her mother's drinking had been more important than her own safety. She decided to spend estate funds to hire a cleaning crew, an auctioneer to dispose of the possessions, and a real estate agent to put the house on the market. "Simply because I could have done all of those things was no reason that I had to," she told a friend. "I had to take care of myself, now more than ever. So I get a few less bucks, so the Humane Society gets a few less bucks. Nothing can compensate me having nightmares again." Knowing your boundaries and practicing self-care is central to reducing the retraumatizing effects of administering the estate of the dead abuser. Sometimes the powerful thing you can do if you've been thrust into this role is open the Yellow Pages or go on Craigslist and hire someone to do parts of the job that could hurt you.

This job can also be empowering as well. Figuring out the balance between empowerment and risk for yourself is a component of self-care after the death of the abusive elder. Marco not only turned his late father's child pornography over to law enforcement. He also worked with his younger sister to collaborate on how to disburse funds that were not specifically designated in the will, using this shared task as an opportunity to bridge the divide that abuse in their family had created between them. Together they made decisions about using their abusive father's estate to benefit children like themselves by making contributions to organizations that assisted abused children. "He thought he was leaving me his shit, but he actually left us some healing." Post-traumatic growth may appear in the aftermath of the abusive elder's death.

So maybe you're not the executor, but you expected to be an heir, and you're not. Or you are an heir, but the amount left to you seems puny in comparison to what your sister got, and you know that she didn't have it as bad as you did. It's not just adult survivors who experience disappointment and anger when a will is read and the bequests seem terribly unfair. In fact, this sequence of events is so commonplace that it serves as the story line for countless plays and stories. Anger at the dead person for how they made bequests, and to whom, is not the sole province of adult survivors. The context of prior maltreatment can enhance the misery, though.

Some adult survivors maintained relationships with abusive elders in the hope of being rewarded with a bequest after their deaths. Some, like Marla, have experienced bitter disappointment and betrayal. If this is you, then you are likely feeling beat up in new and painful ways. This kind of betrayal at the reading of the will is another layer of the death of hope. The adult survivor who has cared for the abusive elder in the hope that his or her service will be recognized in the will has a concrete expression of hope. You were expecting that in death the abusive elder would have become fair and caring and rational in her/his actions in a way that s/he never was in life. Somehow, "think only good of the dead" transforms for some people into "think of the dead as better people than they really were."

Many adult survivors in this predicament will be at risk to blame themselves and chastise themselves for being naïve or foolish. Let me strongly encourage you to do otherwise and to instead redouble your practice of self-compassion. To think well of someone, no matter how badly this person has behaved, speaks to your own decency, and to the survival of your hopeful view of humans despite the misery to which they have subjected you. Practice compassion with yourself, noticing that you are the person who you hoped your elders could be, not the worthless creature they told you that you were. Most people project onto other traits they dislike in themselves, accusing others of venality and cruelty when they are themselves venal and cruel. You, on the other hand, have projected good, seeing your elders as possessed of fairness and care, when the caring and fair person is you.

Dirty Money

On the other side of the room are adult survivors who have assumed, based on the very poor quality of their relationships with the abusive elder, that they would be cut off, and are surprised to discover that they have been left something. If this is you, take a deep breath and sit down. Being the recipient of a financial bequest from the adult who harmed you is no more a totally good thing than is winning a lottery. Money coming from someone who harmed you is the proverbial Pandora's Box. You might feel as if it is simply your due for what you suffered. Or the money might feel tainted because of its source. If the amount is small, you may feel insulted. If the amount is large, you may feel as if you are being offered a posthumous bribe. Sometimes you are enraged that this money is here now, and not when you were little and neglected, lacking for food or clothing, or when you really needed it for therapy ten years ago and the elder refused to help you out.

I have noticed that some of these ambivalent feelings are also common in people who receive damages awards in lawsuits. There is really no amount of money that fully heals the wounds of childhood maltreatment any more than there is an amount of money that completely emotionally compensates people for losing their jobs due to discrimination or their health to medical error. Although the financial windfall does help to pay tuition or your therapy bills, money from the dead hand of an abusive elder can be as wounding as it is healing.

So behave powerfully in your relationship with this kind of money. Proceed with caution. Survivors who have received a financial bequest from an abusive elder have sometimes found it useful to put it aside for a time while they work through, with a therapist, spiritual advisor, financial planner, or other neutral third party, what will feel like the best way in which to spend their inheritance. It matters not how large or small the amount is; one hundred or ten thousand or one million dollars can feel similar when the source is an adult who hurt you, terrorized you, degraded you, neglected you, violated you.

Go back to the boundary-setting section of this book, and pay attention to what you feel, what you want, and what will be healing to you. Ask yourself what the one powerful thing is that you can do right now—and then ask that again the next day, and the next. Notice compassionately your urges to do something reactive to the abusive elder with the money ("I'm going to give it all to the Republican party, that'll make her turn over in her grave"). Notice that s/he is dead, and that the only person who will now have a consequence if you make a reactive decision will be you. Some adult survivor heirs have had fantasies of giving the money to causes that their abuser would have hated, only to realize that in so doing they would still have been in the control of that abusive elder.

Pay attention to what you label this money. It is your money now, but so long as it's "Aunt Reba's money" then you're not coding it as yours in your psyche. Other adult survivor heirs have had the urge to give all of the inheritance away, feeling it to be tainted. Some adult survivors have made the decision to use an inheritance from an abusive elder to cushion their own lives as much as possible, feeling that some of their struggles in adulthood have stemmed from the abuse, and might now be somewhat ameliorated by having additional funds available.

There is no right or wrong thing to do with an inheritance from an abusive elder. Take the time, as much time as you need, to figure out what is right for you. Money is imperishable. It will sit relatively inertly in whatever form you have received it until you are ready and clear about what to do. If you're worried about stocks losing value, pay attention and ask yourself why you're engaging with that topic—what does that kind of worry tell you about what you might want to do with the money, for instance? Get some informed advice about where to put the assets in a form that you can comfortably let sit for as long as you need.

Resist urging even from well-meaning others in your life to do things with it that you do not feel clear about wanting to do. If you've inherited a lot of money, you'll discover how many of your circle of people have good ideas about how you should spend it. Pay attention to your boundaries. You may be feeling guilty about having this money, and that guilt raises your risk of doing things simply to make other people happy so that you will feel safe, a reenactment of old problematic attachment patterns. Know that even once you do have a clear sense of your own goals and desires, your decisions about spending this money will not be simple. Little related to your relationship with the abusive elder has been simple, and living with money you've been left in the aftermath of her or his death is not simple either.

If There's More Than One

For some adult survivors there are only abusive elders in their families of origin. I worked with a woman I'll call Hanna who had been abused in every possible way by every adult who had been responsible for her from the time she was born. Every one of her biological, step, and foster caregivers had done her some kind of harm. Because she was a person with a magnanimous and forgiving spirit who spent many years devoted to healing, she was able to reconnect with one of her biological parents, and to have a caring relationship with him at the end of his life. Her philosophy was that she had to have someone, and that this family member had been the least worst of all of the adults—and that it was good for her to see herself as an adult relating to that person, and to be certain that she could no longer be harmed. That death was one that she was able to grieve as if that parent had been good-enough.

This woman's decisions about how to handle the realities of her life represents one of multiple possibilities for the adult survivor who is dealing with more than one abusive elder's death. As with every other aspect of the death of abusers, there are no wrong or right paths to take.

What is likely to be true if you've had multiple elders who abused you is that you have had different experiences, different feelings, and different relationships with each one of them. You don't need to be fair to abusive elders by responding to every one of their deaths in the same way. After all, remember that these elders were the opposite of fair with you. Being discriminating in your responses is not unfairness. It's honoring your boundaries, and giving yourself the right to respond to each person's death based on what you feel, what you think, and what you know about this person, this death, in this time of your life.

Hanna had never reconciled with her biological mother. She vacillated between hating and despising her for how she had treated Hanna. When her mother died Hanna decided to throw herself a birthday party because "This is my new birthday, the day when the woman who gave birth to me to hurt me died. Today a new person is born, someone who doesn't have a mother who hated her." This contrasted sharply with her real sadness over her biological father's death. Her friends were confused by both of her decisions, but Hanna had made powerful choices in each instance, reflecting the specific relationship she had with each abusive parent, honoring what actions would allow her to continue her healing journey.

Adult survivors who were abused by more than one adult while growing up also frequently carry heavier burdens of self-blame and self-hatred than do other survivors, both of which muddy the process of self-care and empowerment. Aidan kept telling his friends, "What's the common factor here, folks? Let's see. My father beat me up. My mother was way more interested in her needle than me. Stepfathers one, two and three beat me up. Maybe I should have gotten a clue and figured out how to change my behavior." Aidan's core belief, that he was the cause of the actions taken by abusive and neglectful adults in his childhood, took years of therapy and having children of his own to dislodge. His mother died while he was still mired in post-traumatic beliefs about himself. He went to her funeral and praised her as a "good mom despite her flaws."

By the time his father died, Aidan was further along in therapy, less willing to blame himself and hopping mad at the adults who had mistreated him. He decided that the best thing to do was to skip the memorial service and take his children to the zoo, something he had longed for when he was little but never gotten. "I have no grief for that man," he told his therapist. He then proceeded to surprise himself by falling into a deep depression that only lifted as he acknowledged and mourned the death of hope.

Rituals for Death and Healing

Finally, one of the very powerful choices that an adult survivor can make in response to the death of your abuser is participation in ritual. Funerals and memorial services and wakes and shiva are all culturally created and prescribed rituals for helping us to deal with and make some sense of death, and an adult survivor may wish to participate in some of those. Adult survivors can also find it very difficult to be part of the formal ritual process, because of how it assumes the goodness of the dead person, and the sadness of the survivors. For some of you, creating a ritual of your own to honor this passage in your relationship with your abusive elder will be the most powerful choice you can make.

Candace was an ordained minister in the United Church of Christ. When her father, who had been emotionally abusive to her and all of her siblings, died, she asked those siblings if they would feel comfortable with her planning and leading his memorial service. With their support, she developed a service that honored the realities of all of who her father had been—a good friend, a hard worker, a terrible father. "Burying my father was an incredibly healing gift for me; it allowed me to bring together my ministry, which has been so central to me, and my childhood self, from whose painful experience my call to ministry sprang." Very few adult survivors are themselves members of the clergy, although many clergy members, like other helping professionals, are survivors. However, planning and creating a memorial for the dead abuser is something that you don't have to be a clergy person to do.

Alan took a long, solitary hike the day of his older brother's funeral, with a bottle of Ed's favorite beer in his pack. Ed, who had been a practicing alcoholic and died of cirrhosis of the liver, had been a confusing person in Alan's childhood. "He was the one who introduced me to the joys of the wilderness. But he also beat me so badly that I needed stitches, more than once. When he wasn't drinking he was a joy to be around, but when he was drunk he was a scary monster." Alan hiked to a ridge, where he opened up the bottle and poured it out on the ground. "I need to keep the good that I got from him, because he was the only father figure I had. And I need to let go of the bad, because if I hang onto it it's going to be hard for me to stay sober myself." When the abusive elder has been, as Ed had been, a mixture of loving and frightening, that person's death may evoke the desire to do or say something that honors the good as well as the abusive. It's important to know that you can do that, and that you're not being a hypocrite or falling back into denial. The elders who abused you were, as we've discussed before, confusing and complicated figures in your life because they were so often those mixes of violation and love, degradation and nurturance, terror and delight. These are parallel, not only conflicting, truths.

Laurie sat shiva, the Jewish seven-day grief period, at her own home, far from where her family of origin lived, after her mother, who had sexually abused her, died. She told her friends from synagogue that it was important to her not to lose her right to participate in an important ritual of grieving—"That's something I will not let her take away from me." She used this period of time to meditate on the question of how she could deepen her self-care and her commitments to her recovery from sexual abuse. She also did some grieving for her relationship with her family of origin, which had become extremely rocky once she confronted her mother with what she had done. She also decided to recite Kaddish, the prayer said by mourners, at synagogue each day during the ritual grieving period, even though as a daughter with brothers she had no ritual obligation to do so. "Saying Kaddish means I have to be with people, and I can be acknowledged as someone who's grieving a loss. When the Rabbi calls for mourners to stand up for Kaddish, I'll be standing, visible to the congregation. I deserve that acknowledgement, even though the loss I'm grieving isn't the one that most people think I am."

When There Is No Contact

For some adult survivors, this entire book will feel somewhat moot. You have permanently and thoroughly severed contact with your family of origin. You have made a decision that any contact, no matter how slight, with the elders who abused you, or other family members who have enabled or excused that behavior, will be detrimental to you. You have not simply employed a cut-off. You have taken time and energy to figure out that this is the best of several terrible options that you can take. This option is another difficult one among all of the difficult choices for survivors. It usually signals that the abusive elder has continued in her/his behaviors well into your adult life. You have probably made this decision not simply to protect yourself, but also to ensure that your own children or partner are not exposed to someone whose behaviors have not modulated, or have even worsened, over time. There is, nonetheless, grief and its complications when that abusive elder dies, particularly when that elder was a parent.

Belinda was completely estranged from her family of origin, where all of the adults had been abusive in some form or another. She had learned of her mother's death only accidentally, when an acquaintance from high school found her on a social networking site and offered condolences for a loss that had happened over a year previously. Belinda was confused at her own response. "I felt sad, then glad, then relieved, then sad again. Mostly it was like a weight lifted off my shoulders. Finally, finally, I knew she could truly never hurt me or anyone else again, and that's a good thing. The world is a better place because she's not in it." Belinda, like some adult survivors, had done the emotional equivalent of divorce from her family of origin. She had worked hard in her twenties and thirties to find some redeeming value in her parents, and had come to the conclusion that there was none. She had severed the relationship on the heels of having spent a number of years in therapy and having made one last attempt at reconciliation that concluded with her father attempting to assault her.

David's memories of his father sexually abusing him returned when his four-year-old son told him that "Grampy" had "kissed me on my penis." The flood of memories frightened David, and for several months he felt completely uncertain as to how to make sense of what he was learning, but he knew one thing to be true. His father had sexually abused his own son, and protecting that child from any further abuse was paramount in David's mind, no matter what might have happened to him.

When he was finally feeling psychologically centered enough to call his father and confront him about abusing Drew, he was shocked at the response he got. "Yes, and so what. Your grandfather did it to me, and I did it to you, and no one's been the worse for it." David realized that his father's view of sexual abuse was hideously distorted and dangerous, as well as that his father had no idea that he had no memory of his own abuse experience until Drew's disclosure.

With the support of his wife and therapist David told his parents that unless and until they got therapy to address this terrible legacy of abuse in the family that they would have no further unsupervised visits with Drew, ever. David was even more shocked by the response to this boundary, which seemed to him to be a reasonable one that would allow his parents to visit their grandchild while protecting Drew from further abuse.

His parents both became verbally abusive with him and told him that he was being influenced by his therapist's suggestions that sexual "contact," as his father called it, was always harmful. "We've consulted an attorney about whether we can sue your therapist for inflicting emotional distress on us," was the last message David got from his parents.

David, reeling under these emotional blows, made the decision that he could no longer have contact with his parents or other members of his family of origin who had been calling and emailing him to persuade him to relent and "let Drew have his Grampy." He sought the advice of an attorney, who urged him to give his therapist the identifying information about his father necessary to make a child welfare report on the abuse of Drew, which he did, knowing that this would be the final blow in the relationship with his parents. He told his therapist, "You know I haven't given you the information to make the CPS call on my father until I was sure that this was irredeemable." David and his family have had no further contact with his parents since that time. Several years after the estrangement he did a ritual of grieving for his parents, who had died to him during the terrifying months after Drew made the disclosure of abuse. When their actual deaths occurred years later he noticed only that he was glad not to have them out there in the world any longer.

So for some of you, the death of the person who harmed you will be a relief, and that only. Your hope will have died long ago, and you will have done the work of burying it. Like David, you may have felt your abusive elders to be already dead to you. You will feel no need to memorialize the loss of this person because for you it is not a loss of anything but a burden. You may even feel a sense of joy and lightness that the person who hurt you so badly is dead. While this resolution to being abused as a child sounds hard-hearted to some people, it's a resolution that echoes just how hard were the hearts of the abusive elders when they were hurting a child decades ago. Hard hearts can merit hard hearts in return. Sometimes the most powerful thing an adult survivor can do when an abusive elder dies is tell the truth about your anger, and allow it to be the period at the end of the sentence of the abuser's life.

See You in the Afterlife?

For many people, life after death is a very real thing. If you are LDS, you look forward to an eternity in the Celestial Kingdom, reunited with your family. If you are Hindu, you expect to reenter the world in a new form in which you have the chance to work through your failings from this and previous lifetimes. If you are a believer in these or many other faith traditions, the afterlife is not a metaphor for you. You know that you will see your beloved dead in heaven.

So what does this mean about the elder who abused you? Will that person be there, waiting for you when you die, angry at you for having broken the chain of abuse, for having told the truth, for having empowered yourself for the rest of your life? Or will her or his breaking of faith with the core human commitment to children have consigned the elder to more terrible precincts of the afterlife? These questions about afterlife deserve expert attention. Take them to a clergyperson of your faith who you can trust to hold both the truth of your childhood maltreatment experience and the tenets of the faith, not using one to deny or minimize the other. If you do not already have a relationship with such a member of the clergy, the Faithtrust Institute is an excellent resource for locating clergy of many faith traditions who have a well-developed understanding of abuse in the family context. Its website's address is provided the Resources section.

YOUR TURN NOW

The lives of adults who were abused and neglected as children are not easy ones. As adult survivors, you are faced with the biological, psychological, interpersonal and existential legacies of what was done to you almost every day of your lives. Each of you has had to learn the tasks of having a loving and compassionate relationship to yourself, and healthy relationships with the rest of the world, the hard way. Many of you have had to spend hours and years in therapy recovering from the effects of your childhood experiences. Some of you are still struggling. Others have achieved a measure of equilibrium, happiness, and peace.

There is some good news for survivors and for the next generations. Today, at the beginning of the twenty-first century, there are treatments, both psychological and somatic, that have been shown to work to ameliorate, or even eradicate, some of the painful after-effects of childhood maltreatment. There is no magic pill. Medications can help take the edge off of pain and stabilize mood so that you're more able to do the work of therapy, but they are not panaceas. More than ever before mental health professionals are in the position to offer you psychotherapies that will work, as we learn more both about how abuse and neglect inflict harm, and also how to help its survivors heal. This can be true no matter how badly you've been scarred psychologically.

Some Tips About Seeking Therapy

If you are seeing a therapist, or considering seeing one, be sure that this professional understands how important it is to clients, and to trauma survivors in particular, that you are offered compassion, care, and respect. The research on what makes therapy work says that most of the good outcomes are due to the therapist's ability to form an alliance with you and be on your side. Neutrality in a therapist is usually not helpful for trauma survivors. It would be best if this caring therapist understands that trauma treatment occurs in three stages, with the first focused on creating safety and stability, internally and externally, for the survivor. It would be very good if your therapist knows something about one of the evidence-based treatments for trauma, but knowing one of those treatments is not enough. The relationship component must be present for the therapy to help. The entire burgeoning field of mindfulness-based treatments for PTSD, anxiety, depression, and problems of emotion regulation has turned out to be a rich resource for helping adult survivors to heal.

You don't have to know the whole list of names of trauma therapies yourself, although I have included some information about some of them in the Resources section. If you use the term "evidence-based treatment for trauma" your therapist should know what those words mean, and should be able to offer one or some of those healing strategies to you in the context of a supportive, respectful, compassionate relationship where your safety is paramount. This does not mean that therapy will not hurt sometimes. Feeling old pain hurts.

Therapists should demonstrate through their treatment of you that they understand the core importance of the therapy relationship to survivors in therapy, and be familiar with the idea that relational interventions are non-optional for survivors who are their clients. This means that your therapist will not try to fit you into their model of therapy, but will use that model as a helpful guide in which how you feel and what works for you best take center stage. A good trauma therapist is warm and human while being clean about the boundaries of therapy. You can read my consent form on my website to see what I tell my clients about what to expect from me if you'd like a more concrete idea of what I'm talking about.

Your therapist should also understand something about complex trauma, which is the name that many of us currently working as psychotherapists in the field of trauma now use to describe the multi-systems effects of growing up in abusive and neglectful circumstances. The person who survives a car accident or a hurricane or even a sexual assault occurring in adulthood after having had good-enough experiences in earlier life is unlike adult survivors of abusive childhoods. Survivors of complex trauma have frequently had so many exposures to different kinds of trauma, and so little time to recover from them, at such an early age, that the frameworks by which we understand adult-life, one-time traumas don't entirely help therapists to make sense of the lives of adult survivors. Be sure that your therapist knows something about the kind of trauma you're dealing with, or is willing to get consultation or additional training in order to give you the best possible care.

If you've got a therapist who you like and have a good relationship with who doesn't yet know much about trauma, encourage her or him to get further education on the topic. Many national organizations have in-person and online training in trauma treatment, some of which is quite reasonably priced. Since your therapist probably has to get continuing education hours anyhow, getting some of it on topics that enhance her or his understanding of you is a fine idea. This isn't an unreasonable suggestion for you to make to your therapist. My clients do it with me, and I've grown a lot as a therapist because I've investigated and learned about some of the things they've suggested to me. Therapists of all backgrounds have an ethical obligation to be competent in their work, and getting additional training to work more effectively with trauma survivors can be a component of fulfilling that obligation. A further discussion of finding a therapist is in the Resources section.

Progress in the Battle to End Child Abuse

Another piece of the good news is that the rates of childhood maltreatment seem to be going down. This exciting trend began to appear around the turn of this century and seems to be holding steady as an indicator of decline. For many years it appeared that we were dealing with a problem that would never go away, which felt discouraging to survivors, therapists, child welfare workers, and survivors' other allies. While children are still abused and neglected, this is happening to less of them now than before. The willingness that some of you have had to speak up, take action, and insist that children deserve safety is paying off. This matters. You have changed the world with your courage and your truth.

But the rates of child abuse and neglect are not yet where we all want them to be, which is at zero percent. So let me leave you with a suggestion about ways to be powerful in the world.

Something I've noticed in my work as a therapist is that when people have learned to be compassionate with themselves, and have stopped having nightmares and flashbacks and are generally less plagued by symptoms, there is still one aspect of recovery left to them. This is the challenge of making meaning of life, and creating the possibility of post-traumatic growth. Trauma is a meaning-making problem for anyone, no matter when in your life it happens, and no matter what kind it is. For anyone who's been the target of trauma, the huge question of "Why me?" hangs in the air, invisible but powerful. For anyone who's been abused or neglected as a child, that question can get pretty big. Surviving childhood trauma means that you've had to battle every step of the way to free yourself from the emotional harms done to you when you were most vulnerable. You don't have a good life to try to get back to, as do survivors of adult trauma, because you didn't have one of those good lives in the first place.

Finding a project that makes meaning for your life, and that channels the survival skills that you developed along the way into opportunities for safety and healing for others, is a strategy that many adult survivors of my acquaintance have found helpful. Because some folks try to find meaning-making in the role of a family caregiver, and find that meaning thwarted because they've been thrust into reenactments that they didn't know were there, those survivors have felt more defeated and unable to find meaning.

If this is you, please reconsider that verdict on yourself. You're still here, so you haven't failed yet. Before you read this book there was likely a lot you hadn't considered about what having a relationship with or becoming a family caregiver to your abusive elder would entail. Like many of my clients and friends, you were heading toward the edge of an emotional Grand Canyon with no one putting up the railings. I hope you've started to build and strengthen those railings now. Family caregiving may not be your meaning-making project. This doesn't mean that you can't find something in your life that redeems your suffering and empowers you to become more whole. Consider what you can do to be part of the solution to child maltreatment. There are as many avenues for this as there are survivors. You don't have to volunteer at a camp for abused kids or become a therapist or give money to a child abuse prevention organization. You can simply commit to a life of treating everyone decently, starting with yourself.

Dealing with the aging, illness, and death of the adults who harmed you can be an experience of retraumatization. It can also be one of post-traumatic growth. I invite you to empower yourself to make it the latter to the extent you possibly can. You had no choices as a child about who raised you. You had few choices about how to survive. You have choices now. Identifying your choices, knowing what your inner wisdom tells you, will not always give you perfect outcomes. Each choice you make takes back power in your life—and that is a step closer to becoming whole.

Thanks for reading this book. If you have comments or would like to be in touch with me, you can go to my website, www.drlaurabrown.com, where you'll find a link for this book that will bring you to a comments form. I cannot respond to every comment and question, so don't be disappointed if you do not hear back from me personally. You can decide if the comment will appear on the website, or if only I can read it, by marking it as "private" if you'd like.

Coming to the end of life's road with the elders who harmed you can be a perilous journey. It can also be a voyage of liberation, stripping away the last vestiges of harms done to you and opening doors into new, more empowered ways of being in the world. Take that first step. Listen to yourself, be compassionate with yourself, make the choices that heal and empower you. Allow this last act in the drama of the abusive elder's life to be one in which you emerge with a happy ending. This is your turn for care.

Decision-Making Table for Adult Survivors

Use this table to assist yourself in making your decisions about if and how to participate in family caregiving or relationships with abusive elders.

Question	Answer	Consequences for me participating	Consequences for me not participating	Next Steps
Where am I in the healing process?				
What are my support resources?				
What are my other responsibilities?				
What are my financial resources?				
What are workplace considerations?				
What are gender and cultural considerations?				
What are my elder's care needs?				

RESOURCES

What follows is a non-exhaustive list of resources that I or survivors of my acquaintance have found helpful. Your suggestions about additions to this list are welcome, and may be included in future revisions.

Childhood Trauma and Recovery

- Adverse Childhood Experiences Study: http://www.cdc.gov/ace/findings.htm The ACE Study is the largest (seventeen thousand kids) study of the long-term health and mental health consequences of childhood adversity. Difficult reading, and it helps many survivors to see that their struggles are normal for people who've had their experiences.
- Bass, Ellen, & Davis, Laura. *The Courage to Heal*. This book is one of best resources for adult survivors of childhood sexual abuse. Recently revised to include updates with new research on trauma, it's full of advice from other survivors about how to move from surviving to thriving.
- Boon, Suzette, Steele, Kathy, & van der Hart, Onno. *Coping With Trauma-Related Dissociation*. This book is one that many of my clients who struggle with the effects of complex trauma have found very helpful.
- Davis, Laura. *I thought we'd never speak again*. If you're going to try to reconcile with your abusive elder, this is the one book you must read.
- Gil, Eliana. *Outgrowing the Pain*. This very short book is one that many survivors of my acquaintance have found to be a helpful introduction to the shared concerns of others like them.
- Herman, Judith Lewis. *Trauma and Recovery*. Widely acknowledged as one of the very best books about complex trauma, a concept that the author proposed in this volume.

- Lew, Mike. *Victims No Longer.* This is the brother to *The Courage to Heal*, written for men who have survived childhood sexual abuse. Revised in 2004, this book does an excellent job of addressing the gender dynamics that are particular for male survivors.
- Miller, Alice. *The Drama of the Gifted Child.* This is essential reading for people whose experience was of emotional abuse or exploitation by a caregiver. Miller has a number of other, longer books, but this short volume is a must-read.
- Shapiro, Francine. *Getting Past Your Past.* This is the first self-help book by the inventor of EMDR. Full of ideas based in that trauma treatment about how to heal from trauma.

Trauma and Memory

- Courtois, Christine. *Recollections of Sexual Abuse.* Written for professionals, this book nonetheless does an excellent job of reviewing the research on trauma and memory, and goes into some detail about what can be helpful in therapy.
- Freyd, Jennifer. *Betrayal Trauma: The Logic of Forgetting Abuse.* This brief and very accessible volume lays out the scientific underpinnings of Betrayal Trauma Theory, and helps clarify how we remain in relationships where we are harmed.
- Pope, Kenneth S. & Brown, Laura S. *Recovered Memories of Abuse: Assessment, Therapy, Forensics.* Although we wrote this book for a professional audience, it may be helpful for some survivors who wish to have a more thorough grounding in the science of memory for trauma.

Boundaries

- DeBecker, Gavin. *The Gift of Fear.* This is a wonderful book for many reasons. It's DeBecker's own post-traumatic growth story, which can be inspiring. Equally as important, it's permission to listen to yourself and your inner warning signs.

- Freyd, Jennifer, & Birrell, Pamela. *Blind to Betrayal*. This excellent book is a powerful and thoughtful analysis of how our early experiences can teach us to ignore betrayal and violation. Essential understanding for boundary development.

- Spring, Janis Abrams. *How Can I Forgive You?: The Courage to Forgive, The Freedom Not To*. The title says it all. I've included this in the Boundaries section because I see forgiveness or non-forgiveness as a component of boundary development. Spring does a nice job of exploring the complexities of the forgiveness issue, and is not dogmatic in any direction about what a betrayed person should do. Like her other work, more focused on forgiveness after an affair, but applicable to the issues for many survivors.

Compassion and Mindfulness

- Brown, Brené. *The Gift of Imperfection*. A lovely little book about self-compassion and healing shame.

- Kabat-Zinn, Jon. *Full Catastrophe Living*. This book was many people's initial introduction to the principles of mindfulness meditation. Lots of good advice about how to develop a program of mindful practice.

- Kornfield, Jack. *A Path with Heart*. Another classic book introducing Westerners to Buddhist mindful meditation practices.

- Siegel, Daniel. *Mindsight*. For fans of Siegel's work, this book integrates his research on attachment and brain development with applications of mindfulness practice.

Attachment

- Johnson, Sue. *Hold Me Tight: Seven Conversations for a Lifetime of Love*. Although this book could also go into the relationships section,

I've placed it here because the author, a leader in the development of Emotion-Focused Couples Therapy, does such a great job of explaining how early wounds to attachment and childhood trauma affect adults.

- Siegel, Daniel J. *The Developing Mind.* This book does a nice job of reviewing and making accessible for the general reader some of the last two decades of research on attachment and the development of self.

Death and Dying

- American Association of Suicidology's Survivor Page: http://www.suicidology.org/suicide-loss-survivors This web resource is one of the best for survivors of suicide. Maintained by the AAS, which is the home for research and treatment in the field of suicide, it offers links to support groups and a list of publications reviewed and recommended by AAS, as well as an online newsletter for suicide survivors.

- Brener, Anne. *Mourning and Mitzvah.* While written from the Jewish perspective, the author makes a number of excellent suggestions about how to create rituals for grieving that could be adapted and applied by people who aren't Jewish.

- Didion, Joan. *The Year of Magical Thinking.* Although this is a memoir, I include it here because it is the most emotionally honest book I've ever read about the experience of bereavement.

- Levine, Stephen. *Healing Into Life and Death.* This is one of only many books by Levine, who has worked for decades with people in the midst of dying. His work has been the foundation of my understanding of relating to death and grief.

- Some helpful books written for children about death, which I'm suggesting for survivors who want a sense of what normal grief might be like, are written by Nechama Liss-Levinson, a psychologist and psychoanalyst. Her complete list of books can be found at http://www.amazon.com/Nechama-Liss-Levinson/e/B001JP251C/ ref=sr_tc_ep?qid=1336334851

Relationships and Relationship Patterns

- Graham, Dee, Rigsby, Roberta, & Rawlings, Edna. *Loving To Survive.* One of the clearest explanations of how Stockholm Syndrome can develop in the abusive family context.

- Hendrix, Harville. *Getting the Love You Want.* This is a classic self-help book for couples that does a pretty good job of exploring how childhood patterns lead to problematic adult attachments. The author also offers a comprehensive series of exercises that couples can do on their own to heal those patterns in relationship.

- Lewis, Thomas, Amini, Fari, & Lannon, Richard. *A General Theory of Love.* A charming little volume exploring the ways in which our neurobiology affects our choices in relationship.

- Spring, Janis Abrams, & Spring, Michael, *After The Affair.* While not specific to the topic of this book, many of the issues of betrayal of trust in intimate relationships are ones that some survivors have found applicable to their dynamics with the elders who abused them.

Faith and Religion

- Faithtrust Institute: www.faithtrustinstitute.org Faithtrust Institute is an interfaith organization dedicated to the prevention and treatment of sexual and intimate partner violence using the foundation of religious faith. An excellent resource for locating faith-based information on survivor issues, including for survivors of abuse by clergy.

- Fortune, Marie M. *Sexual Violence: The Sin Revisited.* Fortune, an ordained United Church of Christ minister, is the founder of the Faithtrust Institute. Her work on the interface of religion and trauma may be especially helpful to survivors for whom faith is important.
- Fortune, Marie M. & Marshall, Joretta L. *Forgiveness and Abuse: Jewish and Christian Reflections.* This book draws on the two faith traditions to explore questions of how and whether to forgive abuse by someone in the family.
- Kushner, Harold. *When Bad Things Happen to Good People.* Although not formally a religiously-based book, this classic is very informed by its author's many years as a congregational rabbi. Helpful for people of faith struggling with the "Why me?" questions.

Family Caregiving

- American Psychological Association Family Caregiver Toolkit http://www.apa.org/pi/about/publications/caregivers/index.aspx This website, while primarily a resource for psychotherapists working with family caregivers, is full of useful information for caregivers themselves. Contains the work of APA Past-President Carol Goodheart's Task Force on Family Caregiving.
- Family Caregiver Alliance: http://www.caregiver.org/caregiver/jsp/home.jsp
- This national organization is by and for family caregivers, and contains many very helpful resource links.
- Ken Pope's end-of-life and caregiving web page: http://kspope.com/hospices/index.php. Ken Pope is a wizard of finding resources on every possible topic. This is simply one of the many pages on his website; you'll also find pages there about psychotherapy ethics, animal assisted therapies, caring for special needs animals, and much much more.

Personality Disorders

- Kreisman, Jerold & Straus, Hal. *I Hate You, Don't Leave Me.* One of the first, and still one of the most accessible, books for non-therapists about the vicissitudes of relating to a person with a personality disorder.
- Linehan, Marsha. *Skills Training Manual for Treating Borderline Personality Disorder.* This is the foundational work of Dialectical Behavior Therapy (DBT), whose creator, Marsha Linehan, courageously came out in 2011 with her personal story of struggling with self-destructive patterns in life. If you're a survivor who has difficulty with regulating your emotions, who uses self-harm to soothe yourself, or who has difficult and stormy relationships, the skills in this book can change your life.
- Mason, Paul & Kreger, Randi. *Stop Walking on Eggshells.* This book is a helpful "you're not to blame" guide for people who have relationships with individuals who are personality disordered. While not specifically focused on experiences of survivors with elders, many of its insights are quite applicable.

Restorative Justice

- Restorative Justice Online: http://www.restorativejustice.org/ is an excellent web resource on this approach to finding justice in the aftermath of violation. Although RJ approaches are now mostly being practiced in the criminal justice system in the U.S., the model for amends and reconnection between survivors and those who have violated them is one that can inform a survivor who is attempting to navigate relating to abusive elders.

Memoirs by Survivors

- Burroughs, Augusten. *Running with Scissors.* Growing up in the context of neglect and violation.

- Gray Sexton, Linda. *Searching for Mercy Street.* Gray Sexton is the daughter of poet Anne Sexton. This memoir describes life with an emotionally unstable and unavailable parent.
- Karr, Mary. *The Liar's Club.* Karr's book details the experience of growing up in a family where violation and abuse were commonplace.
- Lyden, Jacki. *Daughter of the Queen of Sheba.* Lyden, a reporter for National Public Radio, writes about being raised by a mother with untreated bipolar disorder.
- Wolff, Tobias. *This Boy's Life.* Wolff's book is a story of the impact of neglect.

Trauma-Related Professional Organizations

- APA Division of Trauma Psychology: www.apatraumadivision. org APA's Trauma Psychology Division publishes a journal and a newsletter, and offers programming at the annual APA Convention. Full disclosure: I am a founding member and former President of this group.
- EMDR International Association: www.emdria.org EMDRIA is the organization of EMDR-training psychotherapists around the world. A referral link for EMDRIA-certified therapists is available on the site, in addition to information about training for therapists.
- International Society for Traumatic Stress Studies: www.istss. org ISTSS is a multidisciplinary, international organization that publishes a journal and newsletter, and offers an annual conference as well as on-line continuing education for professionals.
- International Society for the Study of Trauma and Dissociation: www.isst-d.org ISST-D is the home for research and training on complex trauma and dissociation. It publishes a journal and an on-line newsletter, and presents an annual conference. It also offers an on-line training program for professionals wishing to acquire

competence in the treatment of dissociation. ISST-D has a referral list of therapists.

- Sidran Foundation: www.sidran.org Sidran, in addition to having many written resources for survivors and therapists and offering training for therapists and other first responders, has long maintained a referral network of therapists. You can find information here about Vicarious Traumatization as well

- Generation Five: www.generationfive.org Generation Five's mission is "To end child abuse in five generations."

Finding a Psychotherapist

Many state, provincial or local organizations of psychologists, counselors, and social workers have referral services that are free to the public. You can find your local organization by typing such search terms as your state or city name, psychological association, psychiatric society, social work society, or counselor association, into your favorite online search engine. You can also use the referral resources provided by some of the trauma-related organizations listed above. In addition, there are many commercial websites today that offer lists of therapists.

When choosing a therapist it's important to find out not only what her or his credentials are and whether this person is covered by your insurance, but also how it feels to you to work with this person, and whether or not she or he has an understanding of the effects of childhood maltreatment and abuse. Years of experience may be less important than a therapist's knowledge of trauma and her or his ability to be connected to and compassionate with you. Pay attention to your gut. Any therapist who tells you that s/he has a miracle cure that no one else has is misrepresenting her or himself, because there is no such miracle cure. No therapist should ever suggest a sexual relationship to you, try to borrow money from or go into business with you. No therapist should try to make friends with you outside of therapy, or trade your services for theirs.

Attributes of a Powerful Person

Throughout this book I've invited you to consider how to empower yourself. What follows is a very detailed description of how people can be powerful. I think of power as happening in four ways: Somatic power (in our bodies), Intrapersonal power (in our relationships to ourselves), Interpersonal Power (in our relationships with others and the world around us) and Spiritual/Existential Power (in our capacity to make meaning in life). This is not a prescription; it is an evolving list of ways in which people empower themselves in the world.

Somatic Power

The powerful person is in contact with her/his body; the body is experienced as a safe enough place; accepted as it is rather than forced to be larger or smaller than it would be if adequately nourished. If its size or shape creates a lack of safety for a person, change of size or shape happens in the service of safety. There is connection with bodily desires for food, sexual pleasure, and rest; no intentional harm is done to one's own body or that of others. Does not require the ability to see, hear, walk, or talk, nor is a powerful body necessarily free of pain or illness, nor strong or physically fit. Body modifications reflect moves toward power and congruence, and personal construction of self. There is compassion for one's body.

Intrapersonal Power

The powerful person knows what she or he thinks; thinks critically, can change her or his mind; is flexible, not suggestible, yet open to input. Trusts intuition, and also is able to find external data for validation of intuition; knows feelings as they are felt. Feelings are a useful source of information about the here and now. There is an absence of numbness, and the presence of aliveness. There is the ability to experience powerful emotions, to contain affect so as to feel it and function, to be able to self-soothe in ways that are not harmful to self or others physically, psychosocially, or spiritually

Interpersonal Power

A powerful person is more interpersonally effective than not, can have desired impacts on others more of the time than not; no illusions of control;

forgives self and others, and is appropriately self-protective; differentiated, yet flexible. Capable of forming relationships that work more of the time than not with other individuals, groups, and larger systems; able to create and sustain intimacy, to be close without loss of self or engulfment of other, and to be differentiated without being distant or detached; able to decide to end relationships when those become dangerous, toxic, or excessively problematic; able to remain and work out conflict when that's a possibility; enter roles in life—parent, partner, worker—most often from a place of choice, intention, and desire, not accidentally, although she or he welcomes serendipity and the opportunity to encounter the new

Spiritual/Existential Power

The powerful person has systems of meaning-making that assist with responding to the existential challenges of life, and that have the potential to give sense of comfort and well-being; sense of own heritage and culture integrated into identity in ways that allow for better understanding of self; is aware of the social context and can engage with it rather than being controlled by it or unaware of its impact; has a raison d'etre, and is able to integrate that into important aspects of her or his daily life; access to capacities for creativity, fantasy, play and joy; has a sense of reality that is alive, not fixed and concrete.

ABOUT THE AUTHOR

Laura S. Brown received a Ph.D. in clinical psychology in 1977 from Southern Illinois University at Carbondale, and has been a practicing clinical and forensic psychologist in Seattle since 1979. She is a Diplomate of the American Board of Professional Psychology (ABPP). Her career has included the publication of 10 books for professionals, 140 professional articles and book chapters, and five training videotapes, including two specifically devoted to the treatment of trauma survivors. She has received many awards from her colleagues, including APA's Award for Distinguished Professional Contributions to Public Service, the Sarah Haley Award for Clinical Excellence from the International Society for Traumatic Stress Studies, as well as the Elizabeth Hurlock Beckmann Award for being an inspirational educator. She has taught at universities, and leads workshops around the world on trauma treatment and feminist therapy. In 2000, she was the on-site psychologist for the reality TV show *Survivor,* in Australia. Laura lives in Seattle with her partner, where she has an independent practice specializing in working with survivors of childhood trauma. She founded and directs, pro bono, the Fremont Community Therapy Project, www.therapyproject. org a training clinic serving low-income people. Since 2003, she has been a student of the martial art aikido, in which she attained the rank of brown belt in 2012. You can read more about her at www.drlaurabrown.com

Made in the USA
Coppell, TX
17 August 2020